David Guterson's
Snow Falling on Cedars

CONTINUUM CONTEMPORARIES

Also available in this series

Forthcoming in this series

· DAVID GUTERSON'S

Snow Falling on Cedars

A READER'S GUIDE

JENNIFER HAYTOCK

CONTINUUM | NEW YORK | LONDON

2002

The Continuum International Publishing Group Inc
370 Lexington Avenue, New York, NY 10017

The Continuum International Publishing Group Ltd
The Tower Building, 11 York Road, London SE1 7NX

www.continuumbooks.com

Printed in the United States of America

Library of Congress Cataloging-in-Publication Data

Haytock, Jennifer Anne.
    David Guterson's Snow falling on cedars : a reader's guide / Jennifer
Haytock.
        p. cm.—(Continuum contemporaries)
    Includes bibliographical references.
    ISBN 0-8264-5321-X
    1. Guterson, David. Snow falling on cedars. 2. Washington (State)—In
literature. 3. Japanese Americans in literature. I. Title. II. Series.
PS3557.U846 S6534 2002
813'.54—dc21

                                    2002000886

Contents

Acknowledgements

Thanks to Linda Wagner-Martin for getting me started on this project. I am also indebted to John Carroll University for providing me research support in the form of Eric Meljac, who spent hours helping me find information about David Guterson, his work, and the internment of Japanese Americans. Finally, I am grateful to the University of Illinois at Springfield for giving me time to finish this book.

1

The Novelist

David Guterson was born in Seattle, Washington on May 4, 1956, and he has lived in Washington for all but one year of his life. He was the third of Murray and Shirley Guterson's five children. His father was a criminal defense lawyer in Seattle, and Guterson grew up hiking, duck hunting, and fishing in the Northwest outdoors, particularly in the Columbia River Basin. He attended the University of Washington, where in his literature courses he studied Shakespeare, the English Romantic poets, Jane Austen, Ernest Hemingway, and William Faulkner. It was, he told John Blades in an interview for *Publishers Weekly*, most importantly "the Russian writers—Tolstoy, Dostoyevsky, Chekhov, Turgenev— whose view of life I responded to, powerfully." He married his high school sweetheart, Robin Ann Radwick, and they moved to the East Coast when Guterson enrolled in Brown University's creative writing program. He soon dropped out, feeling the program was "too experimental." He returned to Seattle and received a Masters of Fine Arts in 1982 from the University of Washington, learning how to write from, among others, Charles Johnson, winner of the National Book Award for his novel *The Middle Passage*. Guterson taught English at the local high school starting in 1984 until his success with *Snow Falling on Cedars* allowed him to devote himself full time to writing. He and his wife live on Bainbridge Island in Puget Sound with their four children: Taylor, Henry, Travis, and Angelica.

At the age of 21 Guterson began writing stories and trying to get them published. Like most writers, he received many rejections, but some of his stories appeared in the *Seattle Review*, the *Iowa Review*, and the *Prairie Schooner*. He then assembled ten stories—six previously published, four new—which were published as *The Country Ahead of Us, The Country Behind* by Harper & Row in 1989. In his interview with Blades, Guterson credited Raymond Carver among his influences for the stories. These stories generally address the situations of men at turning points in their lives: boys growing to adulthood, men of middle age dealing with their sons and fathers, old men facing the troubles of age. In many of his stories, Guterson uses hunting or other outdoor activities as a venue for personal revelation. *Publishers Weekly* describes the stories as "tell[ing] how men and boys come to understand themselves, at risk to their happiness." "Opening Day," for example, which was first published as "When the Hunt is Done" in *Sports Illustrated*, has as its narrator a man going duck hunting with his father and his son. The narrator experiences moments of revelation as his relationships with the two other men shift and as he observes the connection between grandfather and grandson. Other stories, such as "Angels in the Snow" and "The Flower Garden," describe a male character's relationship with his wife or girlfriend, relationships often tested by flaws in both characters and by the pressures of life's turning points. His stories are also usually historically grounded, whether by cultural context or specific historical markers, as in "The Day of the Moonwalk." Another important theme for Guterson is male friendships. These relationships often contain elements of mystery and outsider-dom, and, in the cases of both "Aliens" and "Arcturus," suggested or actual homosexuality. *The Country Ahead of Us, The Country Behind* was generally well-received, called "poignantly wry" and praised for its "thoughtful writing and expert dialogue" by *Publishers Weekly.* The *Chicago Tribune* admired the way the collection "sustains its artistic vision of the human experience enfolded within larger realities." Still, the collection is not widely known, despite a re-issuing of the book after the success of *Snow Falling on Cedars.* Guterson also had non-fiction work accepted by such publications as *Sports Illustrated* and *Esquire.* He has written on a wide variety of topics, including planned communities, home schooling, the rights of threatened species, professional sports, and the consumerism exemplified by the Mall of America. His work attracted the interest of *Harper's* magazine, where he became a contributing editor. He contributed a piece called "Surrounded by Water" about the advantages and disadvantages of island life to *The Earth at Our Doorstep: Contemporary Writers Celebrate the Landscapes of Home,* edited by Annie Stine and published by Sierra Club Books.

His essay on home-schooling, prompted by his own experience schooling his children and published in *Harper's,* drew a commission from Mane Salierno Mason at Harcourt Brace to write *Family Matters: Why Home Schooling Makes Sense* (1992)—a work he completed in the midst of writing *Snow Falling on Cedars.* The book relies on his family's own experience even as it covers the home-schooling movement as a whole. Guterson emphasizes the benefits home schooling offers children but also describes the problems home-schoolers face within the community. Reviewers of the book pointed often to the apparent contradiction of Guterson, a high school teacher, advocating home schooling. Guterson, according to the *New York Times'* Timothy Egan, "said he wanted to make a case for home schooling that goes beyond the stereotype of religious fundamentalists teaching questionable lessons to sheltered children." He and his wife have allowed their children to make up their own minds on a year-to-year basis whether they want to attend school or learn at home.

In May of 1994, shortly before the release of *Snow Falling on Cedars*, Guterson published an essay called "Blood Brothers" in *The Los Angeles Times* about his own experience with inter-racial friendships as a boy and the growth of this relationship into adulthood. The friendship began on a basketball court:

> Standing beside a portable blackboard, jumping up and down with a length of chalk in my fist—the odd man out of this particular game—I kept score and hoped someone would injure himself so I might take his place. My thoughts, then, were mean-spirited and self-absorbed, and when a smooth-skinned Asian boy with exotic features suggested I'd made a scoring mistake, I cast in his direction a long stream of curses and described his mother as a bitch. I'd heard this insult used only the day before and, with no understanding of its deeper implications, tried it out in the easy manner of a veteran of such invective. I was 11 years old.
>
> The boy whose mother had been debased neither hesitated nor uttered words. Instead, he efficiently threw me to the ground, where both bones in my right forearm snapped, an incident that would join our lives forever and which forever shocked something out of me—though I remained reckless for many years to come, I chose words more carefully afterward and studied people more closely.

The Asian boy, the son of Tibetan refugees, was made to apologize by his mother, and he and Guterson became friends, though they took different paths in life. His father the Sakya Lama and himself a reincarnated lama, Ani Sakya struggled to find his place in Seattle culture; he played basketball and football but "was at times morose and withdrawn, grappling with the peculiar difficulties of his identity": "I remember him in a rainstorm on the Duckabush River, seated on a rock in the lotus position, subjecting himself to the torrent in silence while I huddled inside a hollow tree." This friendship seems to be a model for Ishmael and Hatsue's relationship in *Snow Falling on Cedars*, from the simple inspiration of the hollow tree to the more complicated issue of an immigrant's search for identity. Guterson recalls that "[o]ur minds meshed uneasily, for mine took pleasure in the straight truths of mathematics and believed only in what could be proved, and his wandered expansively. . . . From him I gleaned some inkling of boundlessness." Thus the friendship with Ani possibly shaped Guterson as a writer: the awareness of "boundlessness," his careful choice of words, and his observation of others came from this relationship and are essential elements of the writing and content of *Snow Falling on Cedars*.

Ani grew up to become a lawyer, and eventually he gave up his Western lifestyle to move to India and volunteer with the Tibetan government in exile. As a lawyer, his role was to help draft the Tibetan constitution, which had to reconcile global (and especially Western) standards for democracy with the principles of Buddhism, which declared the Dalai Lama the supreme political as well as spiritual authority: "To complicate matters, Buddhism asserted that the individual's existence was little more than a temporary illusion, that one's separateness from the universe was a hallucination, while democracy held the individual in highest esteem." This conflict can also be seen in *Snow Falling on Cedars*, as both Hatsue and Kabuo struggle to find peace in a community and a country that fails to understand or appreciate their values. Guterson ends his essay with a description of his own trip to India to visit his friend, his editorial contributions to the Tibetan Constitution, and an examination of the East/West conflict in both the East and the West.

Guterson spent eight years working on his first novel, often getting up at 4:30 in the morning to write before going to work. *Snow Falling on Cedars*, purchased by Harcourt Brace for only $15,000, was published in 1994. Guterson credits Harper Lee's novel *To Kill a Mockingbird* as an important influence on the plot of *Snow*

Falling on Cedars: both novels focus on the role of racial prejudice in criminal investigations of murder and in doing so expose underlying hatreds in their respective communities. Guterson also told Linda Mathews of the *New York Times* that he assigned *To Kill a Mockingbird* to his high school classes because "[i]t always got a strong response, because students have a strong need for heroes of a particular type, someone who represents a set of values." He also often taught Shakespeare's *Romeo and Juliet*, which is, of course, a tale of star-crossed lovers. Another literary inspiration he mentioned to *USA Today*'s Bob Minzesheimer is Gabriel Garcia Marquez's *Love in the Time of Cholera*. Guterson explained that both Lee's and Marquez's novels "drop you into a textured world, . . . make you feel like you're in a good dream, and when it's over you feel wistful." In an article on Guterson, Fritz Lanham of the *Houston Chronicle* described the author as "a rarity among fiction writers in that he starts not with a character or a voice or a situation but with a theme, an idea. . . . [H]e was wrestling with the question of how we're supposed to conduct ourselves in a world so inscrutable and unjust." Guterson was impressed by an exhibit on Bainbridge Island, his home, about the history of Japanese Americans, including the years of World War II. He did his own research: library work, interviews, and transcripts of oral histories. In his interview with Mathews, Guterson suggested that the novel was also influenced by real-life people. Ishmael's father, Arthur Chambers, is based on Walt Woodward, who ran the local paper on Bainbridge Island and took a public stance against the internment of Japanese Americans, and Nels Gudmundsson is roughly based on Guterson's father Murray, a criminal defense lawyer. His inspiration for the island of San Piedro came from the island where he lives. After two false starts (throwing out a total of more than 300 pages), Guterson got started on the track that led to the completion of the novel.

Although the novel sold slowly in hard cover, *Snow Falling on Cedars* was unexpectedly successful. Word of mouth and book groups sent paperback sales soaring. In addition, Guterson won the PEN/Faulkner Award for the novel. In his acceptance speech, he actually derided such awards, claiming they "are invidious and divisive and give writers, an already self-absorbed and envious lot, yet another occasion to inflate with self-importance or shrink in churlish resentment." In the same speech, however, Guterson warned that "Congress is making a sorry mistake if it cuts off funding to the NEA."

After the success of *Snow Falling on Cedars*, Guterson became something of a celebrity. He was, for example, chosen as one of *People* magazine's "50 Most Beautiful People in the World" in 1996. The novel has been translated into at least twenty-four languages, and Guterson has toured the United States — as well as such countries as France, Austria, Switzerland, and the Netherlands — promoting his book. He also worked on the movie version of *Snow Falling on Cedars*, which stars Ethan Hawke and Max Von Sydow. He did not write the script, though he did consult with director Scott Hicks and he has a co-producer credit. The movie, released in the winter of 1999, was not widely popular or well received by critics.

For his second novel, *East of the Mountains* (1999), Guterson traveled throughout Washington state, particularly to the Columbia River basin. He also went to the Dolomites in Italy to research material on World War II. This novel follows the events in a few days of the life of seventy-three-year-old Dr. Ben Givens, who, having been diagnosed with colon cancer, decides to commit suicide. To do so, he journeys east of Seattle toward the apple farms where he grew up, and along the way he meets a variety of people — encounters that permanently change both his life and theirs. Ben's travels are intermixed with flashbacks to his youth on his family's farm, to his relationship with his now-dead wife, and to his experience in World War II; in this way the novel is similar to *Snow Falling on Cedars*, with war experiences being central to who the character has become. The novel's themes include physical damage or illness reflecting spiritual damage; memories of war and violence affecting the present; the influence of nature and place; and redemption, particularly finding the strength to move on after severe losses. Many of these ideas, of course, are extensions of issues Guterson explored in his first novel. Like *Snow Falling on Cedars*, according to reviewer Walter Kirn (*New York*), "[i]t teaches the interconnectedness of all things and the basic goodness of human nature." Guterson himself said in an interview with Minzesheimer that the novel "is about love and work and death and the balance in life between the bleak realities—aging, illness and death—and on the other hand, love and meaningful work and the beauty of this work. It asks a basic question: Why should we go on?"

Despite a strong investment in promotion by Harcourt Brace, *East of the Mountains* was not as well received as *Snow Falling on Cedars*. Descriptions of the land and of places, for example, can be plodding, and unlike similar passages in *Snow Falling on Cedars*, they seem to have less relevance to the structure and meaning of the work. Kirn suggested that the novel's craftedness is "oddly distancing" and that the work is too concerned with conveying "right thinking." *Publishers Weekly*, however, offered a different view: "[Guterson's] unsparingly direct, beautifully observed and meticulously detailed prose creates an almost palpable atmospheric background" (51). Carolyn Maddux, writing for the *Antioch Review*, suggested that the negative reviews *East of the Mountains* received reflected the critics' desire for something more like *Snow Falling on Cedars*, a view shared by Tony Freemantle of the *Houston Chronicle*. *East of the Mountains* is a different kind of novel: a spiritual journey, focused on one man and his memories and his pain, episodic in style; it lacks the suspense and breadth of *Snow Falling on Cedars*, but for readers prepared to take *East of the Mountains* for what it is, these may not be weaknesses at all.

Like many novelists, including his mentor Charles Johnson as well as such writers as Toni Morrison, Margaret Atwood, William Faulkner, Nathaniel Hawthorne, and John Irving, among others, Guterson is concerned with the effect history has on the present and on the possibilities for the future. These authors look to the past, often re-interpreting and re-emphasizing events to challenge our accepted notions of history and of identity. Like Faulkner in particular, Guterson suggests that the past is never past, that the past is always shaping and engulfing the present. He is engaged with cultural memory, stimulating and stirring our perceptions of ourselves and how we ended up where we are.

While not unsympathetic to women, Guterson's writing unapologetically focuses on the masculine condition, recalling most significantly the work of Ernest Hemingway. Stylistically different from Hemingway, Guterson is similarly concerned with how a man defines and faces manhood, particularly in the face of war's challenges to masculinity. For both writers, war — as well as love — provides opportunities that can define or humiliate, the tests of manhood that culture dictates boys face to become men. Guterson's short stories in *The Country Ahead of Us, The Country Behind* explore the problem of masculinity, of how to be a man and live peacefully within American society. These stories evoke those of Hemingway, particularly "The Big Two-Hearted River," "Soldier's Home," "The Three-Day Blow," and "My Old Man;" these stories recount men's pain in the aftermath of war, men's friendships, and father/son relationships. In *The Sun Also Rises* (1926), Hemingway suggests that it is the maintaining of ritual, of "keeping face," of following the code, that proves manhood. Guterson seems to agree to a certain extent (the fishermen in *Snow Falling on Cedars* have a code of silence and autonomy that evokes the Hemingway hero), yet with the character of Ishmael Chambers he implies that the code can be damaging.

The influence of Harper Lee's *To Kill a Mockingbird* on *Snow Falling on Cedars* and other Guterson work is clear. Both Lee's and Guterson's novels show a desire for justice and clarity in light of racial tension when the system of justice is itself infected by prejudice. For both authors, race relations are the flash point, the issue that sparks the difficulty of finding justice. While fighting prejudice is central to both works, the issues of morality raised can be extended to all human interactions. This search for moral certainty in both works is conveyed through the eyes of children, though Guterson's work demonstrates that the quest for rightness and fairness can be just as puzzling for adults.

2

The Novel

Snow *Falling on Cedars* seems, at first, to be the story of the trial of Kabuo Miyamoto, a Japanese-American fisherman, for the murder of Carl Heine, a fellow fisherman who happens, unfortunately for Kabuo, to be white. The present scene of the novel is the courtroom, where Nels Gudmundsson defends Kabuo, Ishmael Chambers covers the trial for the island newspaper, and Kabuo's wife Hatsue watches and suffers. But this immediacy and simplicity of plot soon slide into the past and into events that have led these people to these positions. The "subplots" become as important as the "plot," the past as important as the present. Ishmael and Hatsue's teenage love affair, for example, becomes a medium through which we see the complexity of the island's racism as well as the private emotions that drive both Ishmael and Hatsue in their adult lives. Ishmael's experience during his war service on the Pacific front and the loss of his arm parallel Hatsue's time in an internment camp for Japanese Americans. Similarly, the boyhood friendship of Kabuo and Carl, combined with the revelations of their experiences during war (Kabuo's in particular) and the illegal land deal between their fathers lead to their encounter on Carl's boat the night of his death. As the story weaves through past and present, through different lives, it gradually comes to focus on Ishmael, not to the exclusion of the other characters but *through* them, *to* him, and his quest to find some meaning and comfort in life. The novel leaves us with Ishmael as he imagines what must have taken place between Carl and Kabuo—a creative act that others on the island, because of their racism and in spite of their decency, seem incapable of achieving.

The novel, despite its deviation in form from a standard thriller or courtroom drama, sustains suspense throughout. The tension, however, becomes less that of plot than of character: have or will these people succumb to their personal weaknesses at the expense of others? While at first we wonder if Kabuo killed Carl coldly out of revenge or hatred, we soon come to fear that the racism that pervades the island may have driven Kabuo to murder and, perhaps, justified the act; and that Ishmael, who obtains proof of Kabuo's innocence, will choose to hide the truth in an ill-conceived attempt to regain Hatsue. These possibilities seem less than remote and well within reach of the characters' drives and desires. Thus suspense plays an important part in the novel, even as the text changes our ideas about the kind of tension that propels a murder mystery.

The subplots of *Snow Falling on Cedars* also offer means by which to categorize the book. It has been first viewed as a murder mystery, thriller, or courtroom drama. It could be considered a war novel, as most of the male main characters are veterans and the primary impetus for the plot builds out of racial divisions that have been exacerbated by World War II. The accusation of Kabuo in particular comes from the coroner's prejudiced view of the wound on Carl's head as resulting from a *kendo* blow; military tactics are distinctly racialized and nationalized. The novel spends considerable time discussing the build toward the United States' participation in World War II as well as on Kabuo's and Ishmael's experiences at war. We see the trauma of the battlefield and its aftereffects in the silences of Carl, Kabuo, and Ishmael. All three of these men suffer long after the war and attempt, through their various roles in island and family life, to come to terms with the war, their own actions — whether brave or cowardly — in it, and its effect on the community's racial dynamics. The war, after all, leads directly to Carl's and Kabuo's conversation on the boat, as Kabuo attempts to regain the land his family was in the process of purchasing from Carl's father when the war interrupted, sending all Japanese Americans into forced labor or internment. And it is the war that makes Hatsue see clearly that she and Ishmael not only cannot be together but also do not belong together; war intensifies the cultural differences that separate them. Thus Guterson weaves together threads of genre — thriller, courtroom drama, war novel, romance — in such a way as to produce a work that defies easy classification. The breaking of genre boundaries is one of the most intriguing aspects of the novel.

Snow Falling on Cedars breaks ground in that it brings into mainstream literature an issue often ignored in American writing and by most Americans: the incarceration of Japanese Americans during World War II. Guterson portrays this tragedy by examining its effects on individuals, families, and the entire island community. When the Japanese-American families have their fathers and husbands arrested and taken away, when the women and children are given eight days to pack, when the FBI takes away items of Japanese heritage (a flute, sheet music, a sword, a kimono) and labels them subversive, the enormity and injustice of internment becomes real. When the white islanders silently watch their Japanese-American neighbors loaded onto a ferry, we see how easily underlying resentments become dangerous and how inaction can equal injustice. The fear of the unknown and the drive to contain it can lead to hatred, and Guterson reminds us of the truism that to be ignorant of history is to risk repeating it. His meticulous research — not only on the subject of Japanese-American internment but on all aspects of the novel (berry-picking, fishing, clam-digging) gives the work a sense of truth and depth.

Setting: Place and Time

For a community that lives on an island, place and nature play a significant role. In an interview published in *The Bookseller*, Guterson explains the literary significance of islands: "Islands in history, and in literature and myth, are places of paradise and also sites for leper colonies and prisons, places to which people can be exiled forever." Viewed in this way, islands are both desired and feared, and this dual nature of islands works as an underlying factor in *Snow Falling on Cedars*. Hatsue, for example, dreams of a strawberry farm on the island as a means to contentment and peace. On the other hand, tourists in the street disturb Ishmael because they "reminded him of other places and elicited in him a prodding doubt that living here was what he wanted" (30); like most islanders in the novel, Ishmael lives as his parents did, a kind of entrapment that could be considered exile. People's lives are shaped by what the land is capable of growing and by the opportunities of the surrounding water. Their relationships with each other are carefully controlled in order not to offend, not to make enemies. Ishmael's father Arthur Chambers understands this: "No one trod easily upon the emotions of another where the sea licked everywhere against an endless shoreline. And this was excellent and poor at the same time — excellent because it meant most people took care, poor because it meant an inbreeding of the spirit, too much held in, regret and silent brooding, a world whose inhabitants walked in trepidation, in fear of opening up" (439). Thus, both Arthur and Guterson suggest that place has a profound effect on character: the island causes a reticence and a forcing of distance. At the same time, however, the novel suggests that that distance *is* forced. When Sheriff Art Moran, for example, must tell Carl's wife Susan Marie that her husband is dead, he struggles to find the proper words and manner to convey news that will damage lives:

> Driving up to see Susan Marie Heine, Art muddled out his words in silence, revising as he went and planning his demeanor, which ought, he decided, to have a vaguely military architecture with certain nautical decorative touches—to report a man's death at sea to his widow was a task done gravely but with tragic stoicism for centuries on end, he figured. . . .
>
> But this would not do. She was not unknown to him; he couldn't treat her like a stranger. After all, he saw her at church every Sunday after services pouring tea and coffee in the reception room. She always dressed impeccably for her duties as hostess in a pillbox hat, tweed suit, and beige gloves: taking coffee from her sure hand he'd found pleasurable. (68)

Because he knows her, his plans to keep his distance—not to enter the house, to have someone else call her sister—all fall away. The distance that would have helped him is revealed for what it is: a willful attempt to prevent the pain of too much intimacy.

Just as the island shapes relationships, island life molds their livelihoods and the rhythms of their days: "San Piedro lived and breathed by the salmon, and the cryptic places where they ran at night were the subject of perpetual conversation" (13). Islanders fish or farm strawberries for a living, and work cycles with the seasons. Island life shapes death as well, as Sheriff Moran knows: "It happened now and then to fishermen—they caught a hand or a sleeve in their net webbing and went over even in calm weather. It was a part of things, part of the fabric of the place" (17). Place works itself into relationships as well. Ishmael and Hatsue's youthful, forbidden romance is tied to memories of the ocean, clam-digging, strawberry picking, and a hollowed-out cedar tree. Hatsue marries Kabuo in part, at least, because his skin, like hers, smells of strawberries (89). The island, the life it produces, and the characters it creates are intricately bound together. The relationships that result may, as Arthur Chambers suggests, suffer from an "inbreeding of the spirit," but they also have about them an air of security. Because they know the place, they know each other—not thoroughly or ultimately, perhaps, but enough to provide the comfort of the known.

The weather on the island reinforces the community's isolation and reflects, shapes, and signifies the characters' emotions. Rain is described as "the spirit of the place" (6), suggesting a grim attitude toward life and reflecting a lesson that Hatsue must learn: that there is more to life than beauty (81). The novel opens inside the overheated courthouse, yet it is the view outside the building that fascinates Kabuo Miyamoto and reflects the atmosphere of the trial: "[t]he snow blurred from vision the clean contours of these cedar hills. The sea wind drove snowflakes steadily inland, hurling them against the fragrant trees, and the snow began to settle on the highest branches with a gentle implacability" (5). Like the snow, the issues surrounding Kabuo's trial blur the "clean contours" of the truth, and its "gentle implacability" reflects the quiet but ever-present racism of the island community, a hatred that cannot be faced or avoided. For Ishmael, the weather conjures up a wish for an earlier time, a more innocent existence: "he hoped it would snow recklessly and bring to the island the impossible winter purity, so rare and precious, he remembered fondly from his youth" (8). The storm and its effects are described in a journalistic tone; specific events from all over the island are given, including snowball fights, broken arms, a man slipping, a car accident, school buses taking children home, and the shopping runs at the stores. This tone reflects the inhabitants' stoic acceptance of the storm and its dangers:

This storm might well be like others past that had caused them to suffer, had *killed* even—or perhaps it might dwindle beneath tonight's stars and give their children snowbound happiness. Who knew? Who could predict? If disaster, so be it, they said to themselves. There was nothing to be done except what could be done. The rest—like the salt water around them, which swallowed the snow without any effort, remaining what it was implacably—was out of their hands, beyond. (255)

This stoicism in the face of the storm signifies passivity in response to the circumstantial evidence facing Kabuo; the islanders refuse to fight their racism that leads to a condemnation of Kabuo without hearing or considering his side of the story. As the days pass, for Ishmael the storm and the trial become competitors, and he wonders how the community can worry about the storm's damage while one of its citizens stands trial for murder (313).

Like the weather, the island as a natural object reflects the import of larger events on the island community's life. When, after the bombing of Pearl Harbor and Hatsue's father is taken away, "the woods felt black and the trees looked sodden and smelled pungently of rot" (203), as if even nature understands the unsoundness of the island community's social structure. The rot of racism and hypocrisy bubbles quickly to the surface when the war begins.

Guterson describes the island in specific detail, including two maps at the beginning of the novel that locate the island off the coast of Washington state and that provide the geography of San Piedro island. He also minutely details the island's town and hills and the specific paths that Ishmael and Hatsue use (107). One result of such accuracy is that the reader can picture San Piedro as if it were a real place, where, correspondingly, such events could really take place. The truth of the place enhances the truth of the story. Such precision in regard to geography also enhances the narrative technique (discussed below) of an oscillation between the intensely personal and the more objective, journalistic accounts of events in the novel. Just as the place of the novel is quite specific, so too the historical setting is made quite clear. World War II is one of the obvious time-markers; others include references to the Westinghouse family and the Lindbergh kidnapping (103). It is important that the events of this novel take place during a specific era of American history because it is a specific tale that Guterson tells, showing how specific events such as World War II and the incarceration of Japanese Americans in internment camps can affect specific individuals. To understand it, we, as readers, must be able to place the novel's events with other events that are more familiar. Its specificity puts the story in a time line, one that leads to the present and stretches back to causes and to responsibility.

Narrative Technique

The narrative switches fluidly between present and past and among the events of the trial, individual memories, and community history. In this way, Guterson suggests that memory is a significant part of the individual's sense of self — both personal memory and cultural memory, as Hatsue in particular learns. By intertwining the present and various characters' personal memories, the text becomes the story of a community rather than just a collection of individuals, yet the individuals in that community remain discrete. In addition to the narrative of the present and flashbacks, the text includes reportage, either specific excerpts from the *San Piedro Review* or simply objective passages that present the history of the island. In this way the text becomes a pastiche of information, disruptive of chronological time and leaving the reader to create a chronology. The reader, like the characters, must negotiate a complex world.

People's testimony on the witness stand serves often to project the narrative into past events. When Sheriff Moran is asked to tell the court his story, we learn first about how he became sheriff: "He'd come to his vocation as if driven ineluctably; he had never formed the intention of being sheriff, yet, to his astonishment, here he was" (10–11). This piece of information does not further the narrative of the crime but instead indicates that people are as important as events. Then, instead of hearing the sheriff's story in his words, as the jury would hear it, the narrative takes us back in time to the day he and his deputy found Carl Heine's body. In this way the narrative becomes more personal, as if the story matters only to Art Moran, and at the same time more communal, as if the jury does not need his words because they already know. Nels Gudmundsson's cross-examination, however, is narrated from an objective viewpoint—a more objective third person narrator—in the court room, bringing us back to the present, reminding us of the trial, and opening up questions in the sheriff's narrative that leave us with a sense of greater possibilities and the limitations of individual perception. We receive other information similarly; the testimony of Horace Whaley, the medical examiner, for example, is also told as a narration of events on the day Carl died, then brought to the present by Nels Gudmundsson's cross-examination. The past exists, it can be told, but the memory and interpretation of it can also be questioned.

The testimony of other characters, such as Carl's wife Susan Marie, inspires flashbacks to different points in the past—to her choosing Carl; to their life together, in particular their sex life; and to the issue of purchasing land from Ole Jurgenson. Even as Susan Marie sits in the witness box, the reader learns intimate information about Susan Marie and her feelings for Carl. Because this information is not strictly related to the trial, the narrative suggests the obvious: that there is more to life than this crime and that Carl's death is a personal loss, not merely a plot device. For Nels Gudmundsson, even, the act of cross-examining brings memories of the past; he is embarrassed by his slow movements "because as a young man he had been lithe and an athlete, had always moved fluidly across the floorboards of courtrooms, had always felt admired for his physical appearance" (27). Through these flashbacks we come to know people as well as events.

The novel has been called a "coming of age" story, but the process from youth to adulthood for Ishmael, Hatsue, and Kabuo appears to the reader in fragmented pieces. Even the flashbacks do not occur in chronological order. Ishmael's first memory in the novel is of his time after the war when he went to school in Seattle, and then his story jumps further back, to that of his father. These memories flow seamlessly: Ishmael recalls how he chose journalism over literature, and this leads directly to the story of his father, who was also a reporter. Most of his memories occur late in the novel, however. First Guterson shows us Hatsue's memories, which are triggered by her conversation with her husband, and her flashbacks hint at Ishmael's, which are in turn prompted by his observation of her in court. Thus one story bumps into another, one version fills out the previous one. In one flashback, Ishmael, observing Hatsue from a distance, wonders "if other boys did this sort of thing, if his voyeurism constituted a disease" (105). Kabuo's memories later reveal that he too spied on Hatsue when they were young. Both Kabuo's and Ishmael's stories center on Hatsue, and a three-cornered love triangle develops. The stories exert tension on each other as the novel pushes aside Ishmael's memories for Kabuo's and vice versa. Hatsue, in this dynamic, retains her own individuality and at the same time becomes an object of cultural struggle. Just as she is crowned the Strawberry Festival Princess in an inter-cultural ritual truce, she mediates in the text between the implications of an inter-racial marriage and an intra-racial one; that is, she becomes an object of narrative struggle that signifies the cultural tensions she must negotiate. In contrast to personal and intimate memories, the text at times maintains a rigid third person objectivity, much like reportage. Right after the novel introduces the courtroom scene and Kabuo Miyamoto, Guterson presents the history of the island:

San Piedro was an island of five thousand damp souls, named by lost Spaniards who moored offshore in the year 1603. They'd sailed in search of the Northwest Passage, as many Spaniards did in those days, and their pilot and captain, Martín de Quilar of the Viscaíno expedition, sent a work detail ashore to cull a fresh spar pole from among the hemlocks at water's edge. Its members were murdered almost immediately upon setting foot on the beach by a party of Nootka slave raiders. (5)

This narrative voice assumes objectivity, yet the description of the islanders as "damp souls" indicates sympathy and intimacy with the community. Objectivity and sources that claim to be objective are problematic throughout. Part of the island's history is revealed through articles from the local paper, written by Ishmael's father. These purportedly-objective passages place the events of the story within a historical context, but the reader must remember that even newspaper accounts can be biased. Arthur Chambers has his own political agenda, one sympathetic toward Japanese Americans, and even if his is one of the primary voices of moral accountability, it is still a biased voice. Arthur himself points out to his son that reporters make choices about which facts get printed. In the courthouse during Kabuo's trial, reporters from the mainland loosen their ties and remove their jackets, showing, in Ishmael's view, a disrespect for the proceedings: "Ishmael understood that an air of disdain, of contempt for the island and its inhabitants, blew from the knot of out-of-town reporters toward the citizens in the gallery" (7). As the story progresses, such an attitude becomes even more troubling: we come to learn how public and private events on the island have led to the arrest and trial of Kabuo Miyamoto, events outsiders will fail to understand. Readers become insiders through their access to personal memories, but the reporters do not have such access and the stories they will write will inevitably fail to capture the "truth" of what happened. Indeed, even Ishmael cannot write the truth without the use of his place as an insider, his imagination, and his ability to empathize with the people concerned. His final story is not journalistic reportage but an editorial. Such a questioning, even a rejection, of the idea of objectivity reinforces the difficulty a jury would have in equitably deciding Kabuo's case.

Race and Racism

Racism underlies the novel, provides the impetus for its plot, signifies the differences between people, and even suggests possibilities for renewal and redemption. It is present before the war but made more "necessary" by the war — the need to feel hatred for the "Japs" who seem to be an immediate threat to the island in the aftermath of the bombing of Pearl Harbor. But what is racism in this context? What fear does this racism cover? One of the immediate answers lies in economics; this is the arena in which divisions between races are made most visible and the one that is pointed to as the motive for Kabuo Miyamoto murdering Carl Heine: land ownership. Still, there are deeper cultural conflicts between the whites (of varied European heritages) and the Japanese Americans that make communication and understanding almost impossible. As Guterson explores the issue, racism becomes just as much about cultural conflict and misunderstandings as it does a prejudice against skin color.

IMAGES OF JAPANESE AMERICANS

Kabuo Miyamoto sums up the island's — and the nation's — prejudice against the Japanese and Japanese Americans: "We're sly and treacherous. . . . You can't trust a Jap, can you?" (391). Indeed, white people on the island do not understand why Kabuo did not come forward with his story right away, failing to recognize that their own prejudice prevented him from doing so. Kabuo's summary of anti-Japanese prejudice encapsulates the unique attitude toward Asians — a racism different in its construction than prejudice against, for example, African Americans, suggesting the socially and historically constructed nature of racism in general. Scholar Mary Young illuminates the issue from the perspective of popular culture in the United States throughout the twentieth century. Her essay, "Setting Sun: Popular Culture Images of the Japanese and Japanese Americans and Public Policy," shows that anti-Japanese sentiment in America began with the arrival of the first Japanese immigrants at the end of the nineteenth century:

They possessed all the attributes that Euro-Americans wanted in immigrants: hard-working, intelligent and law-abiding. Yet, according to their detractors, they were racially unassimilable and hopelessly alien in their religion and culture. They were loyal only to imperialist Japan; they were dangerously efficient economic competitors. Also, they had low standards of living, a high birth rate, and "vile" habits. (52)

Japanese Americans also suffered prejudice resulting from American fears about the Bolshevik revolution in Russia and a general antiforeign sentiment after World War I. Popular literature confirmed stereotypes against the Japanese, including such flat and unflattering characters as "the comical servant, sinister villains, the asexual detective, militaristic despots and docile hordes of followers of the emperor" (Young 54). Several of these works, including a short story by Jack London and novels by Homer Lea, Wallace Irwin, and Peter B. Kynes, predicted futures in which China and Japan ruled the world. Movies, too, portrayed the Japanese as treacherous, economically ruthless, and intent on world domination. These popular images, Young shows, had prepared Americans "to view the Japanese as subhuman militarists" by the time of World War II (58), and anti-Japanese images continued in film, cartoons, and songs. Young demonstrates that such prejudicial propaganda continues to the present day (consider, perhaps, the Asian-based economically ruthless aliens in *Star Wars Episode I: The Phantom Menace*).

In *Snow Falling on Cedars*, Etta Heine, Carl's mother, most often exhibits such attitudes. She watches Zenhichi Miyamoto with a resentful eye when he comes to buy land from her husband and reads something sinister into his appearance: "Something he knew about kept him from aging while she, Etta, grew worn and weary — something he knew about yet kept to himself, bottled up behind his face. Maybe it was Jap religion, she thought, or maybe it was in his blood. There didn't seem any way to know" (132). She later complains to her son that Kabuo continually gives her "dirty looks" (138). Etta hates the Miyamotos because she cannot understand them and lacks the generosity to try. While she is an extreme example of racist attitudes, others on the island hold such attitudes in varying degrees, and these stereotypes represent those of the nation as a whole. Ishmael Chambers reflects on the anti-Japanese propaganda fed to him during his military experience. A colonel tells him to "take no prisoners: shoot first and ask questions later. The enemy, you see, has no respect for life, his own or anyone else's. He doesn't play by the rules. . . . It's characteristic of the Jap to be sly and treacherous" (344). It is this propaganda that Kabuo throws back in Carl's face with the repetition of the words "sly and treacherous." Ishmael recognizes that such stereotypes are intended to make American soldiers "able to kill [the Japanese] with no remorse" (345), but he still cannot escape the stereotype when he looks at Kabuo Miyamoto on trial. He knows it is "all propaganda. . . . but at the same time I find myself thinking about it whenever I look at Miyamoto sitting there staring straight ahead. They could have used his face for one of their propaganda films — he's that inscrutable" (344–5).

RACE AND THE ISLAND'S ECONOMY

The text makes clear that race is built into the island's economy as well as its social structure. Americans of European descent own land; Japanese Americans work the land. This is not to say whites do not work hard, for there are many scenes of whites laboring on their land. Ishmael Chambers and Hatsue Imada work in the same strawberry fields, although each picks berries with his or her own group of friends — groups determined by race. Still, to some extent the separation of whites and Japanese Americans works like a land owner/land worker division. The novel provides careful details about the role of Japanese immigrants through the island's history:

Company books preserved in the Island County historical archives record that in 1907 eighteen Japanese were injured or maimed at the Port Jefferson mill. Jap Number 107, the books indicate, lost his hand to a ripping blade on March 12 and received an injury payment of $7.80. Jap Number 57 dislocated his right hip on May 29 when a stack of lumber toppled over. (76)

We see here how, in the early days of their presence on the island, Japanese Americans were de-humanized, referred to by number not by name, and commodified—one hand worth not even $8. This attitude lingers: Etta Heine's first comment on learning that the Japanese Americans are to be interred is a question as to who will work the fields. Furthermore, before World War II American law made it impossible for Japanese Americans to own land by declaring that no Japanese immigrant can be naturalized and that no alien can own land. (Interestingly, Young points out that the prohibition against Japanese owning land was not because they might have taken valuable land away from European Americans but rather because "they took land which was considered valueless by Euro-Americans and consistently produced larger yields on smaller acreage" [53]. Thus the law seems to have arisen out of an American sense of inferiority.) This double bind is one of the driving points of the novel's plot: the Miyamotos want to own seven acres of land, gradually buying it from Carl Heine, Sr., but they lose the land when Carl Sr. dies because the deal must necessarily remain private and is based only on Carl's good will. Regaining this land is, for Kabuo Miyamoto, a gesture of respect for his father as well as an attempt to achieve normalcy after the war.

The divide between the community of owners and laborers is ritually "healed" once a year with the Strawberry Festival, in which a girl of Japanese descent is chosen as the Strawberry Princess, "an unwitting intermediary between two communities, a human sacrifice who allowed the festivities to go forward with no uttered ill will" (78). Noticeably, the Strawberry Princess only forces the "ill will" to remain silent; it is not dispersed or alleviated. This custom also adds gender to the problem of racism. The "human sacrifice" must be a girl; as Gayle Rubin suggests in her classic essay "The Traffic in Women," women often serve as alliance builders between two different groups, irrespective of the individual woman's wishes.

That Hatsue, herself a Strawberry Princess, rejects Ishmael thus has larger implications; she refuses to be the vehicle through which two cultures might come together because she understands not only the personal loss she would face but also the political implications of a marriage between herself and a white man. Her choice of Kabuo is a public rejection of the Strawberry Festival tradition in its wider implications—a choice that reflects a pessimistic view of the future of relations between Japanese Americans and whites.

RACE AND CULTURE

The novel explores the distinct cultural differences between the Japanese Americans and the European Americans on the island, differences that stem more from dissimilar world views than from skin color. Hatsue tells her husband not to be so stiff in court because, she says, he looks like "one of Tojo's soldiers" (80). Yet Kabuo does not intend for his erect bearing to convey guilt for Carl Heine's murder or disdain for the judicial process and the island community; rather he believes, as he was taught by his father, that one must maintain composure at all times and trust one's audience to understand:

That was what his father had taught him: the greater the composure, the more revealed one was, the truth of one's inner life was manifest—a pleasing paradox. It had seemed to Kabuo that his detachment from this world was somehow self-explanatory, that the judge, the jurors, and the people in the gallery would recognize the face of a war veteran who had forever sacrificed his tranquillity in order that they might have theirs. Now, looking at himself, scrutinizing his face, he saw that he appeared defiant instead. He had refused to respond to anything that happened, had not allowed the jurors to read in his face the palpitations of his heart. (154–55)

Kabuo's audience—the jury—has not been raised as he has, not been trained to read in his composure the meaning of his innocence. This cultural misunderstanding has profound dangers for Kabuo, although he, unlike the jurors, is able to read both cultures; he realizes that his "composure" has been read as "defiance." Like many members of minority groups, he can read both the dominant and the minority culture.

Guterson shows that Kabuo's religious beliefs are a large part of this difference. As a Buddhist, he believes in karma and the Great Wheel of life, of things coming back. So when he sits in trial for Carl's murder, he cannot evade feelings of guilt for the murders he *has* committed: "it made sense to him that he might pay for his war murders: everything comes back to you, nothing is accidental" (157). He exudes guilt because he feels guilty, not for Carl's death, but ultimately he sees little difference. The suffering he endures in his separation from his family is, he believes, suffering he deserves: "he would . . . have to accept that the mountain of his violent sins was too large to climb in this lifetime. He would still be climbing it in the next and the next, and his suffering inevitably would multiply" (169). The war, which further divides the members of the San Piedro community, places an extra burden on Kabuo: he must go fight because of his honor but also because he is Japanese. "There was something extra that had to be proved, a burden this particular war placed on him, and if he would not carry it, who would?" (92). Ironically, the murders that Kabuo has committed and for which he feels guilty are those that his society praises by awarding him medals.

Like Kabuo, Hatsue has been taught by her mother and other Japanese women to practice calmness: "Her life had always been strenuous—field work, internment, more field work on top of housework—but during this period under Mrs. Shigemura's tutelage she had learned to compose herself in the face of it. It was a matter in part of posture and breathing, but even more so of *soul*" (83). Mrs. Shigemura, a representative of "old ways," teaches Hatsue calligraphy and the rite of the tea ceremony, but she also teaches Hatsue the difference between the Japanese and American philosophies of life: "In America, she said, there was fear of death; here life was separate from Being. A Japanese, on the other hand, must see that life embraces death, and when she feels the truth of this she will gain tranquillity" (83). Although Hatsue often feels that she has achieved external composure but no inner peace, this outer tranquillity serves her well—just as it serves her mother when her father is jailed. "The trick," Fujiko Imada tells her daughters, "was to live here without hating yourself because all around you was hatred. The trick was to refuse to allow your pain to prevent you from living honorably" (200). This way of living leaves Hatsue incomprehensible to Ishmael, just as Kabuo is incomprehensible to the jurors. Hatsue's affair with Ishmael leaves her vulnerable to the loss of tranquility and of honorable living, in part because her Japanese heritage relies on strong ties to family and community. In her letter to Ishmael's parents after Fujiko Imada discovers her daughter's affair with Ishmael, Fujiko states that "[i]t was no crime to find oneself attracted to another . . . or to believe what one felt was love. The dishonor lay instead in concealing from one's family the nature of one's affections" (229). Hatsue's betrayal of her family is, to Fujiko, her worst crime, but it is a crime not only against the family but also against Hatsue herself. By lying, by excluding her family from an important part of her life, Hatsue has damaged her honor, honor meant to provide Hatsue with strength in the face of trouble. If she cannot maintain that honor, she becomes susceptible to a weakening of the soul.

Race and cultural heritage ultimately divide Hatsue and Ishmael, although the reason for their split is more apparent to Hatsue than to Ishmael. Significantly, Hatsue and Ishmael argue about the nature of the oceans; Hatsue insists there are four, but Ishmael responds that "[t]he main thing is, water is water. Names on a map don't mean anything" (97). Hatsue points out, however, that she has heard that the colors of the oceans are different, the Atlantic brown, and the Indian, blue. This conversation serves as a metaphor for how the two see race. Ishmael prefers to think of all people as people and to ignore racial and cultural differences between them. Hatsue, however, comes to understand that things are not that simple. Cultural heritage is valuable, she learns; it provides strength. She has no wish to erase the differences between herself and Ishmael. Furthermore, Ishmael's disappointment and anger at Hatsue's rejection of him is often framed in racist terms, showing that even he, who professes love for Hatsue, is not immune from the island's — and the nation's — racism.

Although present before World War II, the war makes racism more immediate, more necessary. It becomes a way to defend oneself against the invisible and in many ways intangible threat to personal security and national identity. The islanders, paranoid about attacks by the Japanese, driven by a fear of a change in their world view, intensify their racial attacks after Pearl Harbor. Ironically, the European American soldiers from the island — Ishmael, Carl Heine, medical examiner Horace Whaley — all serve on the Pacific front, while Kabuo fights in Europe. Such an alignment of race with enemy parallels the island's social and economic structure. Ishmael's racism, pain at Hatsue's rejection, and anger at the loss of his arm all are expressed in his invective *"that fucking goddamn Jap bitch"* (250). For Ishmael, race and gender come together as the target for his sense of pain and loss. Carl's anger too is oddly intertwined between personal feelings and public sentiment; he tells Kabuo how sorry he is that his mother sold the Miyamoto land, saying if he had been around it would not have happened, but "I was out at sea, fighting you goddamn Jap sons a—" (404). His sense of guilt for Kabuo's loss becomes twisted with his own personal horrors. Kabuo's response further reveals the irony of the island's racial divide: "Am I calling you a Nazi, you big Nazi bastard? I killed men who looked just like you—pig-fed German bastards. I've got their blood on my soul, Carl, and it doesn't wash off very easily. So don't you talk to me about Japs, you big Nazi son of a bitch" (404). Carl's killing of Japanese soldiers in the war is rendered acceptable because of the racial hierarchy in the United States, but Kabuo points out the double standard.

RACISM AND JUSTICE

In his acceptance speech for the PEN/Faulkner Award, Guterson explained that for him, the novel is "about the fact that we human beings are required by the very nature of our existence to conduct ourselves carefully. It's about the fact that in an indifferent universe, a world full of horrible accidents and inexplicable travail, the only thing we can really control is our own behavior." In *Snow Falling on Cedars*, this sense of justice is stated most clearly by Hatsue; responding to Ishmael's complacency in the face of unfairness, Hatsue says: "I'm not talking about the whole universe. . . . I'm talking about people. . . . People don't have to be unfair, do they? That isn't just *part of things*, when people are unfair to somebody" (326). Although it would be simplistic to say the problems of racism would be overcome by basic kindness, for the San Piedro community, where people are so closely linked, such kindness could effect significant change.

One of the concerns of the novel is the relationship between justice and morality. When Etta Heine responds to Kabuo Miyamoto's anger at the loss of his family's land with the claim that she did nothing wrong, Kabuo says, "You haven't done anything *illegal*. ... Wrong is a different matter" (138). Kabuo indicates that what the law allows is not equivalent to moral behavior. After all, for many years the law forbade Japanese to become citizens or to own land; the law put Japanese Americans in internment camps; the law holds Kabuo for trial based on circumstantial evidence—biased evidence, as the medical examiner tells the sheriff to look for a "Jap" based on his interpretation of Carl's wound through his lens as a veteran of the Pacific theater of war. The novel does not, however, attempt to define morality, beyond Hatsue's plea for fairness. How will this community move on after the trial? Will Kabuo ever gain a place of respect in the community or will he always be looked at as a killer, a sly treacherous "Jap" who got away with murder?

Significantly, the jury is not given a chance to rule on the case. The crucial evidence Ishmael finds saves Kabuo and prevents the community from having to render a verdict. Guterson puts the legal system on trial here, differentiating between justice and the law. The law makes mistakes; Kabuo is saved not by police work or by the skill of his attorney but rather by luck, by the fluke that Ishmael thought to check records of boat traffic when his main purpose was to find information about island weather and by Ishmael's reluctant acceptance of his own responsibility to be decent to another person. Readers, too, are asked to judge, but in addition to the testimony heard in court they know characters' memories and emotions. By adding layers to knowledge, we begin to see that even with our omniscient narrator we still do not know everything; how, then, is a court of law, with its edited and biased information, to be an equitable dispenser of justice?

World War II

The uneasy peace between the races on the island is shattered by the bombing of Pearl Harbor. The readers learn about this event in the novel first through the perspective of the Japanese Americans; we learn when they do, and we follow the immediate reactions and fears of the Japanese Americans. The white islanders move quickly to express their anger and prejudice, unscrewing the light bulbs from Shigeru Ichiyama's movie theater marquee. The war shakes the community as well as irrevocably alters the lives of many of its citizen; the participation of the United States in World War II affects many people besides soldiers. Japanese Americans were interred in camps, disrupting domestic life. When Hatsue's father is arrested by the FBI, his family is told to "think of it as a war sacrifice" (198). Thus the war works itself into the stories of people on the home front as well as of those who go to battle, and in this way the novel is about World War II as much as it is about San Piedro, the murder trial, and the pain of lost love. The memories of war experiences are woven into the structure of the novel as a whole.

AT THE FRONT

Snow Falling on Cedars shows how World War II alters the men who fought in it. Their experience of violence has left them feeling separated from the people around them. The flashbacks to the characters' military service are integral parts of the narrative, explaining both how the characters have been shaped and how, subsequently, they come to view their present lives. For Ishmael, for example, the war has changed the world in ways he cannot even

explain: "People appeared enormously foolish to him. He understood that they were only animated cavities full of jelly and strings
and liquids. He had seen the insides of jaggedly ripped-open dead
people. He knew, for instance, what brains looked like spilling out
of someone's head" (35). These memories of violence separate him
from others and prevent his becoming emotionally attached or in-
vested in any person or thing. He cannot "feel what God is" (342)
and realizes only with surprise that he will miss his mother when
she dies. As his mother says, he "went numb" (347).

The description of Ishmael's military training is, ironically, immediately preceded by the description of Hatsue and Kabuo's first
kiss. This linkage of events suggests the on-going connection for
Ishmael between the war and Hatsue's rejection of him. The pain,
fear, and anger he feels all seem bound up in his loss; when he falls
ill, for example, "it began to seem to him strangely apt that he lay
so many thousand miles from home and was so alone in his sick-
ness. It was the kind of suffering, after all, he'd yearned for during
the last five months, since receiving Hatsue's letter" (234). His time
of training is suffused with detachment; he follows veteran soldiers'
example of drinking and indifference to their practice maneuvers.
Like the others, he writes a last letter home before battle, but his is
to Hatsue and in it he describes his unending hatred for "Japs" and
for Hatsue herself: "He explained to her the nature of his hatred
[for the Japanese] and told her she was as responsible for it as
anyone in the world" (237). Although Ishmael does not send this
letter, it nevertheless conveys the extent to which his personal feelings of loss have become entrenched in a wider system of prejudice
and hatred. When his platoon is bombed during their attack on the
South Pacific island, one of his fellow soldiers identifies it as a
"fucking Jap shell" (241), as if the national origin of the shell
somehow made it more deadly.

The confusion that ensues during Ishmael's experience on the island is typical of many soldiers' accounts of battle. Before he even leaves his ship, he finds himself wondering about his purpose: "He had listened to Lieutenant Pavelman as closely as he could but had not discerned the relationship between his words and the specific direction in which his own feet should move once he landed on Betio. Why was he going there? To do what exactly?" (240). The waters are choppy, the battle is mis-timed, the squad leader is killed almost immediately, and the ocean turns red with men's blood. Having lost his equipment during the landing, Ishmael finds himself "unarmed and without a job to do" (245). Here he is eventually confronted by a sergeant who

berated them relentlessly, a stream of invective, characterizing them as "the sorts of cowards who ought to have your balls chewed off real slow and painful-like when this goddamn battle is over," men who'd let "other men do the dirty work to save your own sorry asses," men who "aren't men at all but cornhole-fuckers and jack-off artists with half-inch hard-ons on those days once a year when you can get your sorry dicks to stand at half-mast." (246)

The sergeant's rant ends only when he is shot, and the episode challenges stereotypical notions of masculinity, suggesting that such images of men without fear doing heroic deeds are based more on wishful thinking then on the actualities of battle. Men faint and vomit. Ishmael's role during this battle is mainly that of a spectator; he gets himself to safety and watches while other men land and are shot. Though finally prodded by a lieutenant into action, Ishmael feels himself caught in a "dream in which events repeated themselves" (249). He spends nine hours waiting for medical corpsmen after being shot in the arm, and then he finds himself one of many boys lying in rows on the ship. The experience of the military and of battle attacks Ishmael's sense of manhood, of reality, and of individuality. Having lost Hatsue and experiencing the horror of the actuality of war rather than "the war moment little boys are prone to dream about" (243), Ishmael's illusions about life are shattered. Carl Heine too goes to war, though we learn little about his experiences except that he fought at Okinawa — a fact that impresses his fellow fishermen to the extent that they cannot believe he died in a simple fishing accident. The battle for Okinawa in April 1945 was the largest amphibious operation in the Pacific war and became a two-month battle of attrition, with heavy losses on both sides, including a large number of Okinawan civilians. The purpose of capturing the island had been to provide a staging area for a larger invasion of Japan, but, ironically, such an invasion was never necessary. That Carl was involved in this battle suggests that he too, like Ishmael and Kabuo, saw horrors and lives wasted. He brings this horror home inside him. One of his primary reasons for getting back his family's land is his need to get off his boat, because the boat and the ocean remind him of "the *Canton* going down, men drowning while he watched" (297). The war placed him, like Ishmael, in the position of an on-looker, unable to change the course of events, and this helps explain his later desires to build his own house and to regain his family's land: actions inspired by the need for control.

Kabuo Miyamoto volunteers for war service; despite his new wife Hatsue's objections, he feels that fighting is something he must do to maintain his dignity. Thelma Chang's "*I Can Never Forget*": *Men of the 100th/442nd* provides historical background for the experience of Japanese Americans in the armed forces during World War II. Only 1,250 men of draft age in the internment camps — out of 23,000 — volunteered for service, and of those only 800 were accepted. Kabuo, therefore, is an exception, in an historical context.

Furthermore, the 100th/442nd, the regiment in which Guterson places Kabuo, lost two-thirds of its soldiers in a month, and by contextualizing his experience in this way Guterson indicates Kabuo's courage and his skill as a soldier—as well as his good luck. Chang's book describes the racism Japanese American soldiers encountered and the prejudice they faced even after the war. With this information, we see that Kabuo indeed displays deep courage and loyalty to the country that incarcerated him and his family and that in all probability he faced some of the fiercest fighting of the war. His memories confirm and personalize his experience of violence; in particular he remembers the German boy whom he shot and who begged Kabuo to save him (153). This memory is something he cannot escape—something he does not necessarily want to escape:

The world was unreal, a nuisance that prevented him from focusing on his memory of that boy, on the flies in a cloud over his astonished face, the pool of blood filtering out of his shirt and into the forest floor, smelling rank, the sound of gunfire from the hillside to the east—he'd left there, and then he hadn't left. And still there had been more murders after this, three more, less difficult than the first had been but murders nonetheless. So how to explain his face to people? (154)

Like other war veterans, Kabuo is left haunted by terrible memories and has no way to communicate his experience.

VETERANS AND COMMUNICATION

The war experience has changed Ishmael, Carl, and Kabuo by creating in them a kind of silence; they are often unable to communicate, especially but not only about their war experiences. Kabuo feels that he lives life "underwater" (153), and Carl tells his wife that "since the war he couldn't *speak*" (297). Both Carl's and Kabuo's wives realize there are dark places in their husbands that they cannot reach. Susan Marie Heine recognizes that Carl cannot explain, that "there was a part of him she couldn't get to" (295). Hatsue feels that Kabuo's war experience is "the crucial fact of her marriage" (359). These men have seen horrors and committed horrors; Ishmael thinks that "after the war the world was thoroughly altered. It was not even a thing you could explain to anybody" (35). As veterans of other wars (World War I, Vietnam— see such fictional accounts as Ernest Hemingway's A *Farewell to Arms* and Tim O'Brien's *The Things They Carried*) have discovered, words no longer have the capability to convey meaning; there are no words to describe what they have seen and done and felt (or do not feel) because their experiences are so far outside of the mainstream, so far even out of their own previous understanding of the world. Ishmael also finds that no one wants to listen; no one wants to hear war stories. Only Hatsue expresses sympathy for his lost arm; other people on the island refuse even to acknowledge that his arm is gone. Perhaps her own experience in the internment camps has given her a degree of insight into the mind of the veteran, although she often finds her own husband inscrutable. Like many veterans Ishmael, Carl, and Kabuo find a wall between themselves and noncombatants. Their understanding of the world has changed, irrevocably.

Carl and Kabuo both marry, and they both return to their old way of life, fishing and farming. These occupations seem to suit them: no talking is required for the solitary fisherman or farmer. In fact, as fishermen their silence is an asset: "On San Piedro the silent-toiling, autonomous gill-netter became the collective image of the *good* man. He who was too gregarious, who spoke too much and too ardently desired the company of others, their conversation and their laughter, did not have what life required" (38–39). This image of the *"good* man" recalls the "code hero" of Ernest Hemingway, himself a veteran of World War I. The *"good* man" and the "code hero" are both expected to be self-sufficient, strong, and silent, and the recurrence of this image from World War I literature to World War II suggests something about the horrors of war: that in post-war life, veterans desire rules to compensate for the lack of rules during war and one must prove one's strength by standing in isolation. In *Snow Falling on Cedars*, the island community's insistence on maintaining personal distance suits men in their post-war lives particularly well. Although they have not made peace with the past, they have found ways to cope.

Ishmael, like the others, returns to the occupation of his father, but unlike the others, his occupation requires communication, and thus tension arises between his profession and his personal desires. Even before the war, however, he has difficulty with words: "He himself was always in need of words, even when he couldn't quite muster them" (111). Now that he makes his living by writing, however, words have a more central role than they do for other veterans. Still, he functions much like they do, silent and distant, and his lost arm and his war years gain him access to the taciturn fishing community. He discovers, near the end of the novel, that instead of doing great things with words that he has used them as a shield, "burying himself in whatever was safe" (442). He finds he must break free of this safety, not only to prove to Hatsue that he still has admirable qualities but also to realize the extent of his being, to reach beyond safety to something more powerful. Thus, at the end of the novel, Ishmael sits at his typewriter, attempting to discover in his imagination the story of the island's trial and to convey this story back to them. His restraint in his life, his desire for safety, is at the end abandoned, as he "[gives] himself over to the writing of it" (460). This writing is a breakthrough for Ishmael; it shows an interest outside himself and his pain and provides an opportunity for him to create something positive instead of dwelling on the destruction (of his relationship with Hatsue, of his comrades, of his arm) that had previously driven him.

THE INTERNMENT OF JAPANESE AMERICANS

Before discussing the representation of the internment of Japanese Americans in *Snow Falling on Cedars*, a brief overview of historical events is helpful in order to understand the broader context in which Guterson's characters are situated. Roger Daniels' essay "Incarcerating Japanese Americans: An Atrocity Revisited" provides the demographics of the United States at the time of World War II:

According to the census of 1940 there were almost 127,000 persons of Japanese birth or ancestry in the continental United States, constituting less than one-tenth of one percent of the population. Some forty-seven thousand of these were persons who had emigrated from Japan before 1925 and were, like other Asians, ineligible for citizenship. . . . The nearly universal prejudice against people of color was the chief cause of discrimination in America, but for Japanese Americans there was the added factor of the trans-Pacific rivalry between Japan and the United States. . . . And, after war came, Americans were much more hostile to Japanese than to German soldiers. (118)

Although, as Daniels points out, the U.S. government was concerned about repeating the crimes against German Americans that occurred during World War I, it was far less effective in protecting the rights of Japanese Americans (119). White Americans feared Japanese espionage, fears fed by the media, but in fact no espionage cases against Japanese Americans were ever brought forth (Daniels

120). Fear on the West Coast was particularly strong, since aircraft factories were located in that area (121).

Public sentiment, media pressure, and governmental forces built steadily until, on February 19, 1942, President Franklin Roosevelt signed Executive Order 9066, which authorized government agencies to provide areas of seclusion to any persons deemed a threat to national security. The order did not name Japanese Americans specifically; indeed it could have been used against large groups of German Americans and Italian Americans on the East Coast but was not. Daniels describes the process by which the first Japanese Americans were incarcerated; significantly, the first order applied only to the small Japanese-American community on Bainbridge Island in Puget Sound—the island on which Guterson now lives and which he used as a model for San Piedro. According to Daniels, "[t]he Bainbridge Islanders, given five days notice, were ordered to report to the ferry slip on March 29, bringing only what they could carry. . . . The [islanders] were surrounded by soldiers armed with bayonetted rifles, ferried to the mainland, loaded onto railway carriages, and shipped more than 1,000 miles to Southern California" (123). Soon afterwards the internment of Japanese Americans began on a wide-spread scale.

Guterson's depiction of the relocation of Japanese Americans is well-researched, and we see the harshness and inhumanity of the internment. Although in the novel the community is given eight days to pack and in reality they were given five, the essentials remain the same. In *Snow Falling on Cedars*, the San Piedro Japanese Americans are loaded on to the ferry and then taken by train to a transit camp—horse stables converted for this purpose (217). The use of horse stables indicates a deeper feeling toward Japanese Americans, a lack of recognition of their humanity. Manzanar, the camp in which the San Piedro Japanese Americans are interred, was located about two hundred miles from Los Angeles, in the middle of the desert. For the islanders, the dryness and dustiness of the camp is a kind of torture in itself. The conditions, the humiliations, the physical sufferings, and the lack of control make all the inmates "like ghosts" (220). Life in the internment camps proved detrimental to the values and way of life of many Japanese Americans. In her study, "Survival Behind Barbed Wire: The Impact of Imprisonment on Japanese-American Culture During World War II," historian Nancy J. Gentile describes traditional Japanese life as translated to the United States:

> The role of family and community were undeniably important in the socialization of the Japanese-American people. In these two institutions, children learned patience, proper manners, etiquette, respect, deference, and human sensitivity. The parent/child relationship (Koko) reinforced the importance of parental respect, family honor, and community obligation. ... This structure also emphasized a hierarchical family and community scale based on position, gender, and age. Members were taught to know their place and behave accordingly. (17)

Life in the camps, Gentile shows, disrupted most if not all of these foundations. Fathers, like Hisao Imada in Snow Falling on Cedars, were sometimes arrested and taken from their families even before the family arrived at the camp, leaving their wives to take charge of the family—a violation of the patriarchal family structure. Even if families remained intact, fathers could not fulfill their obligation to support their family, since the War Relocation Authority provided food and shelter for their children and wives. Individuals could work, but men and women were paid equally for the menial labor they were permitted to do—again, an overturning of the Japanese-American structure that placed men's work higher on the scale than women's (Gentile 22). The older men, often immigrants (Issei), were not permitted to run for offices in the camp's self-government;

this meant the younger generation (*Nisei*) had authority over their elders — another disruption of Japanese-American culture. The anxieties created by living in overcrowded camps undermined the traditional Japanese strong sense of community. Gentile discusses the memoirs of an internee, Yoshiko Uchida, who described how "pressure from the imprisonment compounded by the short supplies brought out the 'base instincts' of many of the internees, causing them to think only of themselves" (20). Similarly, on the train, Hatsue's mother Fujiko loses sympathy for her fellow travelers, especially for a family with a crying baby: "she secretly began to wish for the baby's death if such a thing could mean silence" (218). This loss of sympathy for others, brought on by forced intimacy and competition for supplies, tore at the strength of the Japanese-American community.

Further, as Gentile shows, internment camp life did not permit the privacy so valued by Japanese Americans, undermining people's dignity. Families lacked their own, protected space in which to bond and to continue Japanese traditions. For example, in *Snow Falling on Cedars* the Imada rooms lack a ceiling, so that the family can hear and be overhead by strangers. On their wedding night, Hatsue and Kabuo cannot escape even the ears of Hatsue's family. Oral histories recount experiences similar to that of Hatsue and Kabuo — newlyweds put into cramped spaces with no privacy from strangers (Gentile 20). Although families were allocated space within larger barracks, as we see with the experience of the Imadas, bathrooms and the mess hall were communal spaces. In Guterson's novel, we see Fujiko suffering the humiliation of the lack of privacy: "Through all of it Fujiko maintained her dignity, though she'd felt herself beginning to crack while relieving herself in front of other women. The contortions of her face as she moved her bowels deeply humiliated her. She hung her head as she sat on the toilet, ashamed of the noises her body made" (217). With the loss of privacy came also a disruption of crucial time with family that allowed them to forge, strengthen, and maintain bonds.

While Hatsue's sisters run wild and their mother often does not know their whereabouts, even at mealtimes (221), the Imadas of *Snow Falling on Cedars* do not seem to experience the destructive effects on family to the extent that Gentile describes them. In fact, it is at the camp that Hatsue openly accepts her Japanese heritage, follows her mother's authority, breaks her previous habit of secrecy and discusses her relationship with Ishmael, and finally marries a Japanese-American man. It is as if, for Hatsue, the threat the camp poses to her heritage makes her value it more, for the Japanese system of community support is made most apparent in the camp. Kabuo and his friends come by to make furniture for the Imadas, simply because they are all from San Piedro. Their island link seems even to strengthen their bond; the closeness fostered by island living perhaps makes the San Piedro Japanese Americans more impervious to the disruptive power of the camp. Hatsue and Kabuo's marriage is based, in part, on their desire for the same thing—a strawberry farm on San Piedro—and on a shared background: "Kabuo was rooted there just as she was, a boy who understood the earth and the working of it and how it was a good thing to live among people one loved" (90). Gentile, in fact, concludes that

the [Japanese-American] group's traditions, customs, and values remained strong enough to help the internees survive the trauma of imprisonment. Respect and admiration for nature persisted in their culture, as did the importance of education and religion. According to historian Edwin O. Reischauer, Japanese culture promoted a strong awareness of the beauty of nature and respect for the environment. (27)

This emphasis on the beauty of nature may be another explanation for Hatsue's strength throughout her internment, as she has memories of the island on which to draw.

Individuals and Relationships

Although the San Piedro community is extremely interdependent, Guterson highlights the isolation of the individual, often by detouring the narrative through a particular character's life and mind at a time when he or she is most emphasized as a member of the community, such as when they are on the witness stand during Kabuo's trial. Although the novel does have main characters — Ishmael, Hatsue, Kabuo — the narrative shines its light on many community members, dipping into their minds and memories, often about very intimate things. For example, as Susan Marie Heine takes the stand, the narrative details her sense of her body, her breasts, and her sex life with Carl. We learn about their marriage, her understanding — or lack thereof — of Carl's relationship with Kabuo, and the tension between Etta Heine and her son over selling the Miyamotos their seven acres of land. Similarly, we learn about Nels Gudmundsson's impotence and his problems urinating — information that seems to have nothing to do with the plot yet establishes a kind of secret connection with the reader. Individuals stand out like gems, glowing and bringing the novel to life.

These individuals are basically decent human beings; Nels, for example, moves away from Kabuo and Hatsue in the courtroom so they can have a few minutes of privacy. He insists Deputy Abel Martinson do the same, and even though Abel claims he cannot disobey orders, he "sidled back about three feet anyway and pretended not to be listening" (80). Only Etta Heine, Carl's mother, has no redeeming qualities and displays outright racism. This does not mean the rest of the islanders lack responsibility for the trial, for they are all to certain degrees complicit in the racial tensions of the community; whether they remove light bulbs from a theater marquee owned by a Japanese-American family or simply watch as their

neighbors are removed to the internment camp, the novel suggests
that they are all implicated in the events that lead to Kabuo's arrest
and trial. In this way Guterson demonstrates one of the dangers of
racism: that we might not recognize it even as we participate in it,
that we can be decent people and still fail to see how our actions
and beliefs constitute an unfairness to others.

In *Snow Falling on Cedars*, father/son relationships demonstrate
the complicated nature of cultural and personal legacy. Ishmael's
father Arthur Chambers, also a journalist and a war veteran, leaves
behind him a valued role in the community's moral life: "Arthur
became an astute and deliberate vegetable gardener, an inveterate
observer of island life, and gradually a small-town newspaperman in
the truest sense: he came to recognize the opportunity his words
provided for leverage, celebrity, and service" (33). Part of his service,
when World War II comes, involves printing editorials that speak
against racial prejudice, a stand that loses him many customers and
requires cutting back the number of pages he can print. Ishmael
feels that while he might try to be as "morally meticulous" as his
father, he is hindered by "this matter of the war—this matter of the
arm he'd lost" (35), ironically failing to consider his father's own
service in World War I. Arthur did not lose any limbs, but like any
World War I veteran he would have seen horrors and lost his
illusions, just as his son does in World War II. This link is one that
Ishmael does not explore, even though his mother points out to
him that both father and son have the same "cynicism:" " 'He loved
humankind dearly and with all his heart, but he disliked most
human beings,' she'd told Ishmael. 'You're the same, you know.
You're your father's son' " (36).

Despite his resistance to replacing his father, particularly as the
island's conscience, Ishmael must learn important lessons about
social responsibility from his father. He once accuses his father of
being biased, of not sticking to the facts, and his father asks him,

"But which facts?. . . . Which facts do we print, Ishmael?" (188), pointing out the false myth of facts equaling truth, that the sifting, sorting, and choosing among facts can be an almost unconscious but still biased process. Arthur Chambers recognizes this and prefers to be open about his biases. He puts the enlisting of Japanese-American islanders on the first page, for example. During Kabuo's trial, Ishmael finds himself in a position to influence public opinion similarly—or at least in a position to point out the islanders' prejudice. Hatsue, in this case, functions as Ishmael's conscience, arguing that the trial itself is unfair and that "[p]eople who can do things because they run newspapers or arrest people or convict them or decide about their lives. People don't have to be unfair, do they?" (326). Ishmael's resolution, at the end of the novel, is to sit and think: he imagines what must have happened that night out on the water between Kabuo Miyamoto and Carl Heine and how it came about that Carl was swept overboard by the wake of a passing ship. To do this, however, he must first spend time in his father's study, looking over his father's books and reflecting on who his father was and what he wanted. He looks at a picture of his father and studies his "cordial, lonely, persevering face" (438). Sitting in his father's study, he remembers that his father "hoped for the best from his fellow islanders, he claimed, and trusted God to guide their hearts, though he knew them to be vulnerable to hate" (439). This combination of affection, respect for individual will, and knowledge of human fallibility is something Ishmael discovers he shares with his father: "Ishmael understood, sitting in his father's place, how he'd arrived at the same view of things" (439). What Ishmael does not realize so overtly is the influence of his mother over both his father and himself; her spirituality, kindness, and sensitivity give both men room to be who they are.

For Kabuo Miyamoto, the father's legacy is, like Ishmael's from Arthur, one of honor. Learning composure, for example, comes from his father. Kabuo's skill at *kendo* is part of his family heritage, from being taught by his father to the weapon he uses that had once belonged to his great-grandfather. But this is a complicated heritage: the great-grandfather had been an "angry man" (166), and after he sees his own violence during the war, Kabuo comes to fear that this anger as well as his skill have been embedded in his blood: "[t]he story of his great-grandfather, the samurai madman, was his own story, too, he saw now" (168). His practice of *kendo* is one of the direct links the police and coroner make between him and the dead man, and his pursuit of his family's seven acres provides the authorities with a motive. His father's legacy, then, puts Kabuo in direct conflict with the community to which his and his father's dreams tie him.

Friendships are irrevocably affected by the war and its accompanying institutionalized racism. Before the war, Kabuo Miyamoto and Carl Heine played together, and Kabuo gives Carl his fishing rod when he must leave for the internment camps. Whether this friendship would have withstood the test of adulthood had the war not interfered is a relevant question; Carl's father seems to be a kind man, willing to work across racial lines to help the Miyamotos buy the land they want. His mother, however, is viciously racist and objects to selling land to Japanese Americans. From this background Carl might have grown either way. Yet his discomfort with Kabuo and his willingness to sell him the Miyamoto seven acres suggests that he retains feelings of friendship for Kabuo, even as Kabuo shows those childhood bonds by insisting Carl keep his fishing pole. Both friends, after all, have followed similar paths in life: island boys who married island girls, who had children after the war, and who make a living fishing while they work to return to strawberry farming. Through the view points of both wives we see similar incidents of family outings on the water, linking the Heine and Miyamoto family lives. But the two men cannot escape the discomfort of racism, exacerbated by the war that allows each to say to the other, "I killed men who looked like you." Part of the tragedy of Carl's death is the loss of a friendship that seems ready to bloom again.

Hatsue and Ishmael's relationship is built on shared childhood memories, of digging clams and picking strawberries. For Ishmael, the fact that their relationship begins when they are so young signals that their love was meant to be; for Hatsue, however, it means that what she feels is not truly love. As a Japanese American, Hatsue must negotiate a much more difficult road to her identity, to knowing who she is and what she values:

[Ishmael] was as much a part of her life as the trees, and he smelled of them and of the clam beaches. And yet he left this hole inside of her. He was not Japanese, and they had met at such a young age, their love had come out of thoughtlessness and impulse, she had fallen into loving him long before she knew herself. . . . And she thought she understood what she had long sought to understand, that she concealed her love for Ishmael Chambers not because she was Japanese in her heart but because she could not in truth profess to the world that what she felt for him was love at all. (205-6)

Her time with Ishmael in the hollow of the cedar tree is like "hibernating at the heart of the forest with time suspended and the world frozen" (208); in contrast, after she marries Kabuo and he departs for the war, she feels that she is "in the stream of history now" (93), a member of the adult, public world. This distinction reflects the novel's own duality: it addresses public events — the trial, the war, internment — even while it explores the inner lives of its characters. Hatsue's choice, then, to join "the stream of history," the public world, suggests that it is the public world that can shape the inner world; she insists that Ishmael write an editorial about fairness not only to save her husband but also because she has a strong sense that the public world matters as much as the private and further, that the public and the private should, to some degree, coincide.

Ishmael Chambers: Loss and Redemption

The novel is about a community, but its recurring focus is the character of Ishmael Chambers: his coming of age, his losses in love and war, and his search to salvage something from what he feels is the wreckage of his life. Ishmael is essentially a kind boy, a kind man—a boy who enjoys the simple pleasures of living on the island and a man sensitive enough to worry that the photograph of a car overturned in the snow might embarrass the car's owner if it appeared in the newspaper (319). This moment tells us much about Ishmael: despite his cynicism, deepened since the war, he has a core of caring left, and he must find a way and a desire to keep this core alive. He has discovered that grief "attached itself and then it burrowed inside and made a nest and stayed. It ate whatever was warm nearby, and then the coldness settled in permanently" (346). But his mother, he notes, has found a way to enjoy life despite the permanent presence of grief over his father's death. She enjoys such small, daily activities as reading, gardening, and talking with friends. He asks her what to do—how to get on with his life—but she cannot provide an answer; it is a question he must resolve on his own.

Named after the narrator of Herman Melville's *Moby Dick*, Ishmael faces some of the same problems. Melville's Ishmael finds himself trapped on a ship captained by the mad Ahab, who is searching relentlessly for the white whale who stole his leg. Reading *Moby Dick*, Ishmael notes that his namesake "was all right, but

Ahab he could not respect and this ultimately undermined the book for him" (31). Ishmael Chambers must find a way to differentiate himself from his own Ahab, who takes several forms: the community that would allow him to condemn Kabuo unjustly, the bitterness resulting from the war, and his own drive to recover Hatsue. He must find a way not to drown in the trial that is the community's witch hunt, their white whale. He is implicated in this hunt, however, by his presence as a white member of that community and his initial refusal to speak out against the racism and injustice underlying the trial. He must also find a way to recover a sense of hope and purpose in life without Hatsue; he must find a way to let her go. His wish for a hug from her seems tied to a wish to escape his guilt at participating in World War II, most particularly in the racist hatred feeding the violence. Her refusal forces him to face his losses on his own. Significantly, Ishmael respects Melville's Ishmael, the sole survivor and thus the storyteller, suggesting that he will, at some point, find peace with himself and that this peace will come through the process of story-telling.

Kabuo's trial for murder is a personal trial for Ishmael as well as a public trial for the San Piedro community. Ishmael, though he discovers crucial evidence that could exonerate Kabuo, waits to pass on what he knows, as if he intends to let Kabuo be convicted and then win Hatsue back. He must overcome his passion for Hatsue, the combination of love and hatred. In a way, he must give up his personal desires and make himself useful to the community as its conscience, as his father was before him and as Hatsue now asks him to be. Further, he must overcome his understanding of people as merely "animated cavities fully of jelly and strings and liquids" (35) and attempt to look inside people, even if he knows that "[t]he heart of *any* other, because it had a will, would remain forever mysterious" (460). Still, he must try, for the effort is what will redeem him. Ishmael's mother points out to him that in his judg-

ment of Kabuo he is "allowing himself an imbalance" (345), refer-
ring partly to Ishmael's lack of journalistic objectivity but also to the
imbalance he has carried within him since the war and since Hatsue's rejection. Ironically, her words invoke the Buddhist sense of
balance that defines the Japanese-American identity; Ishmael must
become more like them in order to heal. And with his subordina-
tion of his personal desires to the greater good, he gains the possi-
bility of finding happiness for himself.

The final words in the novel of both his mother and Hatsue to
Ishmael are the advice to get married and have children. While this
answer seems simplistic, both Carl Heine and Kabuo Miyamoto
have found a degree of peace in marriage and children; having a
wife to share their grief eases their pain, if only a little, and having
children grounds them in the present and the future, rather than in
the past. Both wife and children offer opportunities for love and for
thinking beyond himself. But is this answer applicable for Ishmael?
First, he must re-evaluate how he sees himself and what he values.
Part of this re-evaluation takes place through Hatsue's eyes, for he
re-reads her letter "and understood that she had once admired him,
there was something in him she was grateful for even if she could
not love him. That was a part of himself he'd lost over the years,
that was the part that was gone" (442). Immediately after this discovery he recognizes his own love and need for his mother, realizing
that he has acted as if the relationship does not matter. His acknowl-
edgement of his love for her and the loss he will feel when she dies
is part of his path of growing up, of moving beyond the cedar tree,
of turning what he knows over to the authorities. Finally, the novel
leaves him imagining Kabuo and Carl's story and setting out to
write it, suggesting that for Ishmael grounding himself in the larger
community and in the imagination may be a more fruitful road to
redemption.

3

The Novel's Reception

Reviewers generally praised *Snow Falling on Cedars*, especially for its unique handling of an established genre, its emotional and moral complexity, dense detail, and sophisticated structure. Susan Kenney, writing for *The New York Times Book Review* in October 1994, called the novel "a densely packed, multifaceted work that sometimes hovers on the verge of digressiveness, but in Mr. Guterson's skilled hands never succumbs to the fragmentation that might well have marred such an ambitious undertaking." She proclaimed the book a "finely wrought and flawlessly written first novel." *Time* magazine called *Snow Falling on Cedars* "a beautifully assured and full-bodied story." The novel also received acclaim from such publications as *The Washington Post, The Los Angeles Times, The Booklist, The Chicago Tribune,* and *USA Today. The Washington Times's* Carol Herman described the novel as "Earl Stanley Gardner collaborating with D. H. Lawrence to produce a novel with extravagantly suggestive, poetic language." She also linked the story to Perry Mason, and with these comments she points to one of the novel's interesting strengths: its appeal to both literary critics and to the average reader, a book that reaches both "literary" and "popular" audiences. Paul Sussman made the same point, claiming that the novel "[weaves] strains from both classic and populist American literature into a fruitful and gloriously original whole." *Snow Falling on Cedars* went on to win a number of awards that reflect both critical acclaim and popular embrace: the PEN/Faulkner Award for Fiction, the Barnes & Noble Discovery Award, and the Pacific Northwest Booksellers Award. It was also nominated for the adult trade ABBY award by the American Booksellers Association in 1995.

In the British Isles, criticism was also favorable. Writing for *The Independent*, Sussman described the novel this way: "If, by some extraordinary confluence of time, fate and nautical misfortune, Truman Capote, Arthur Miller, Harper Lee and John Grisham all washed up on a desert island together; and if, once there, they decided to collaborate on a book, they might well come up with something like this." Andrew Biswell, in a review also published by *The Independent*, called *Snow Falling on Cedars* "a novel of substance, tackling large themes on an impressively wide canvas." Nicci Gerrard, a reviewer for *The Observer*, compared the book's melancholy overtones to those of Virginia Woolf's *To the Lighthouse* and J. D. Salinger's *Catcher in the Rye*. *The Herald* (Glasgow)'s Harry Reid suggested that the novel offers "resonances for Scottish readers, for the parallels with certain communities in the Highlands of Scotland are undoubtedly there." Beyond the specific geographic and communal themes of the novel, overseas critics and readers have found something in the novel with which to connect, as *Snow Falling on Cedars* has been translated into over twenty-four languages.

Not all reviews were unmixed, however. Reid indicated disappointment in the lack of humor in the novel and wrote that "the one episode describing action from the Second World War jars . . . the author seems to adopt a different voice here, more strained, more macho, less assured." Several critics pointed out that with so many characters passing through the story, it was difficult for readers to identify with one. Stephen Henighan, reviewing the novel for the *Times Literary Supplement,* felt "[t]he story lacks an intriguing protagonist," indicating about Ishmael Chambers only that he "is the most fully realized character." The *Manchester Guardian Weekly's* Jane Mendelsohn interestingly argued that Hatsue Imada is the real center of the book: she "gives *Snow Falling on Cedars* a life-affirming, unneurotic quality which is absent from so much fiction." Mendelsohn also called the novel "rich with detail, well-constructed, virtuous, and utterly predictable" — predictability, of course, being problematic in a murder mystery. In an article about Guterson's second novel (*East of the Mountains*) entitled "Snow Falling on Readers," *GQ's* Thomas Mallon attacked *Snow Falling on Cedars* for its sentimentality and predictability, calling it "a p.c. police procedural that has been padded out 150 pages past its necessary length." Most critics, however, found depth, complexity, and originality in the work and indicated that Guterson's first novel promised more good work to come.

Many reviewers recognized the extensive research on which the novel is built and praised the work for its powerful use of detail and its complex structure. The *Chicago Tribune's* Nancy Pate, for example, wrote that "Guterson's prose is controlled and graceful, almost detached. But the accretion of small details gives his story weight." Pico Iyer, a reviewer for *Time,* suggested that "Guterson's particular gift is for description: he takes you into one fully researched scene after another — gill-netters at work, an autopsy, digging for geoduck clams." The *Sunday Times* pointed out that Guterson's "practical and sensuous detail" shows the novel's world to be "richly imagined." Biswell similarly described the novel's detail as one of its strengths: "There is no deadweight, and no such thing as incidental detail." Henighan disagreed, writing that "while every detail in this first novel feels credible, few surprise or astonish.

Snow Falling on Cedars suffers from a throttling of the imagination by particulars." He seems to be in the minority, however, as the power of Guterson's language is one of the most-praised aspects of the book. Sussman described the language of *Snow Falling on Cedars* as "mesmeric, quasi-biblical prose." The result of Guterson's way with language and detail is a work of fullness and sensitivity to pacing, as many critics acknowledged. Reid, for instance, pointed out the contrast between the novel's topic of a murder trial — its relation to the thriller and the court-room drama — and the "leisurely, thoughtful pace" of the book's prose. He further praised Guterson for his ability to mix paces, sometimes building "strong narrative momentum" in contrast to the slower, more descriptive moments. *Newsday*'s Laurie Muchnick made a similar point about Guterson: "He is a thoughtful and patient writer. There is no headlong rush to an answer as there would be in a thriller, even the literary kind that's been so popular the past few years. There's room for digression." The flashback structure of the novel was acknowledged as intricate and effective. Muchnick calls the technique "clever," and Kenney described this organization of material and plot as "past events told from the numerous characters' points of view with all the detail and intensity of lives being lived before our very eyes." Sussman indicated that the flashbacks are a way to establish a "tangled collective history." The flashbacks are not the only variation on narrative technique that caught reviewers' attention; Biswell found the passages that come from the San Piedro *Review* to be a way "to bring the idea of journalistic disinterest under scrutiny."

Critics also often described the novel's language and structure in comparison to a television show or film. Henighan called the courtroom scenes "narrated with camera-eye impartiality" and compared the flashbacks to "cinematic dissolves." Iyer described the novel as "movie ready in its pacing and narrative vividness." Similarly, Sussman suggested the flashbacks are kinds of "extended snapshots of the past." And, of course, the novel was actually made into a film; for further discussion, see the next chapter. Despite its cinemagraphic technique and complex structure, *Snow Falling on Cedars* maintains what Michael Harris (the *Los Angeles Times*) described as "a stately pace and an old-fashioned omniscient voice;" the mixture of complex structure and "old-fashioned" tone make the novel simultaneously original and comfortable in its familiarity.

One of the issues reviewers addressed is the problem of genre. *Snow Falling on Cedars* was first, and often still is, regarded as a thriller, courtroom drama, or murder mystery, and many of the reviews reflect this view. Dennis Dodge, writing for the *Booklist*, commented that the novel creates a private trial for Ishmael paralleling the public trial and that the book "is compellingly suspenseful on each of its several levels." Harris suggested that the novel is both a "whodunit" and a "mystery, something altogether richer and deeper." Herman went further, claiming that "Guterson takes what appears to be formulaic crime and trial fiction and turns it on its head. . . . For these violent, court-centered times, the novel is a canny, literate, passionate alternative to the current media extravaganzas where justice, as a concept, seems to vanish." Other critics seemed to view the work as a war novel. Lucy Hughes-Hallett, in a review for the *Sunday Times*, claimed outright that "this is not a courtroom drama" and that "the novel's real subject is an international one, the unquantifiable but dire after-effects of war." Kenney praised the book for combining genres and resulting in something more powerful:

Unlike many recent purveyors of courtroom calisthenics, Mr. Guterson does not stop there. Taking us back nearly a dozen years in both historical and personal time, he depicts the Allied invasion of the South Pacific island of Betio through the eyes of the 19-year-old Ishmael, as, lying gravely wounded on the beach, he sees the rest of his company wiped out, so that like his namesake he alone survives to tell the tale.

Mendelsohn called the novel "[p]art courtroom drama, part sea yarn." Finally, although the novel is also part love story, few critics seemed to address that aspect as a definitive issue. Hughes-Hallett was an exception, calling the teenage, mixed-race romance the "emotional centre" of the novel.

A common focal point for reviews was the novel's treatment of racism and morality. In her review, Pate focused on racial discrimination, showing that "[p]rejudice takes many forms: the outright venom of Etta Heine; white fishermen joking that they can't tell one Japanese-American from another; islanders passively watching as their neighbors are loaded on ferries in Amity Harbor." Harris too boiled the novel down to moral questions when he wondered, "[h]ow can so many good people coexist with a major historical evil? The mystery remains even after the puzzle is satisfyingly solved." Critics tended to agree that the novel ends optimistically but without naivete; Gerrard, for example, said that "what Guterson unsentimentally gives us is a warm-hearted novel, in which life is hard, cultures conflict, but people are essentially well-meaning and stoical on their island in the snow." Iyer called the novel a "tender examination of fairness and forgiveness." Many critics believed that one of the strengths of the novel was the delicacy with which racism is portrayed. Henighan calls Guterson's treatment of the issue "effectively low-key," meaning that Guterson avoids preaching or easy answers but instead develops characters as real people rather than stereotypes to convey the complexity of racism and racist communities. *The Washington Post* similarly said that "Guterson . . . maps out the difficult topography of the islanders' complicated relations with one another, their hidden jealousies, resentments, and suspicions, and their surprising if unreliable capacity for generosity of spirit." Hughes-Hallett also expressed this view: "Guterson is not a sentimental optimist.... His rendering of small-island life is enriched by his awareness of meanness and jealousy as well as by his respect for his characters' strengths." Only a few critics looked more deeply at some of the roots of racism that the novel unearths. Iyer insightfully pointed out that "when the reticent descendants of samurai meet laconic Scandinavian fishermen, one form of silence glances off another." Sussman extended this idea further: "In the book's heart, however, lies less a story of cultural conflict as one of cultural redemption." He wrote, "There are forces greater than those of history, Guterson tells us, and the chains of the past need not be unbreakable."

The novel was praised too for its treatment of a topic long ignored by literature and by Americans: the internment of Japanese Americans during World War II. Herman wrote that "[Guterson] retrieves an important, if bleak, part of this country's history, and he does it not as a lawyer or a visionary, but as a reporter." Most critics, however, failed to explore the implications of Guterson's treatment of Japanese-American internment, often merely mentioning it as part of the plot.

Most critics agreed on the strength and complexity of Guterson's characters. Harris, for example, suggested that it is character that drives the action of the novel: "Just as Miyamoto is obsessed with getting back the exact acreage that his family lost, so Chambers sleepwalks through life in the vague hope of reclaiming Hatsue. The contrast between these two obsessions—one conscious and potentially fruitful, the other unconscious and debilitating—is Guterson's main device for leading us into the mystery." Fritz Lanham of the *Houston Chronicle* acknowledged that *Snow Falling on Cedars'* "real strength lies in its characters, who nurse physical and psychological wounds dating from the war years." Kenney too considered the characters' war damage highly significant and added that "[t]he community [Guterson] conjures up is various and vital. His bit-part players are as engaging and clearly delineated as his principals." Of course, not all critics agreed that the characters are compelling, as Henighan's review, quoted above, shows.

The novel's title too is a topic discussed by most critics, with varying interpretations. Pate compared the snow to the quiet but ever-present racial divide on the island: "The snow quietly blankets the island—much like the silent prejudice that shrouds its 'five thousand damp souls'." Sussman viewed the title as a metaphor for nature's indifference to the pettiness of humans: "Human history, however, is not all. Cedars leaf and fall irrespective of human endeavour, and snow tumbles whatever the disposition of Man." Herman viewed "the accumulating, and then the melting of snow [as] a metaphor for getting to the truth of Kabuo's guilt or innocence and for uncovering the larger question of one community's sense of justice." She also pointed to Hatsue's reflection on "the dark side of life" as equally real as the light side, just as the cold of winter is just as real—or just as illusory—as the heat of summer. Iyer provided yet another interpretation of the title, a metaphor for cultural conflict: "*Snow Falling on Cedars* is poised at precisely that point where an elliptical Japanese delicacy meets the woody, unmoving fiber of the Pacific Northwest." Kenney read a moral lesson from the title: "the mystery plays itself out, along with the storm, leaving the human heart to shake free, as the hardiest cedars shake free of snow, of the chill of hatred and war—if it only will." Muchnick viewed the title as a metaphor for the process of reading itself: "Like the snowfall that is its constant refrain, *Snow Falling on Cedars* builds up gradually, steadily, surrounding the reader with its magic."

4

The Novel's Performance

PUBLICATION AND SALES HISTORY

With an initial printing of 25,000 copies, *Snow Falling on
Cedars* went through twelve printings in five weeks when the paperback version was released in October 1995. The novel spent 37
weeks on *Publishers Weekly*'s best-sellers list and a total of 46 weeks
in the list's top three slots. The paperback version was on the *New
York Times* best-selling list for over a year. The novel also spent
some time at the top of the London *Times* best-selling list. As of
October, 1996, according to *Publishers Weekly*, the novel was Vintage's best-selling paper novel ever and required new printings almost every week. There are currently over four million copies of
the novel in print, and it has been translated into more than twenty-
four languages.

The success of *Snow Falling on Cedars* reveals much about the
marketing and selling of novels in the 1990s. *GQ*'s Thomas Mallon,
though not at all endorsing the book, made an interesting point
about the novel's sales pattern:

Historians of publishing are likely to remember David Guterson's fantastically best-selling novel *Snow Falling on Cedars* as the first Oprah book. They would be wrong—it never received Winfrey's imprimatur—but the mistake will be understandable. . . . Oprah's picks tend to get an astonishing second wind after they've been dying, or at least sleeping, on the shelf. In Guterson's case, it was a PEN/Faulkner Award that finally got the ball rolling into a word-of-mouth avalanche.

Suzanne Mantell's article "The Rise of 'Snow': HB, Vintage, others boost Guterson novel," which appeared in *Publishers Weekly* in December of 1995, describes the factors that combined to create the success of the novel. *Snow Falling on Cedars* received favorable pre-publication reviews and more praise when it was released in October of 1994. Guterson told Mantell that publishing the book just before Christmas helped sales: "It's a good Christmas book because of the title and the cover picture." Sales slowed down until the spring, when the book received the PEN/Faulkner Award, as well as several others. Winning this award was significant for sales because, as Mantell explains, "the PEN/Faulkner Foundation, at Vintage's request, had designed an attention-getting prize sticker for use on the paper edition." The novel sold quickly in the American Northwest, especially in Seattle, San Francisco, and other western cities. Guterson's writing teacher Charles Johnson (*The Middle Passage*) wrote a blurb for the book (and was also one of the judges for the PEN/Faulkner Award). Vintage, the novel's publisher, and its parent company, Harcourt Brace, worked to promote the book, and so did Barnes & Noble. The book mega-chain awarded *Snow Falling on Cedars* its second annual Discovery Award—an award for books by new authors—and placed it in a feature section in its stores. The novel's success is also attributed to word-of-mouth and especially to the growing establishment of book clubs. Vintage, like many publishers, caters to the book club community by providing web pages with reader's guides and author biographies (http://www.randomhouse.com/vintage/read/snow). One book club, the Literary Guild, purchased rights to the book and printed a copy for its members. Guterson himself has helped boost sales by touring the United States and abroad.

The novel's rise to success has not been universal or uncontroversial. In November, 1999, the *New York Times Upfront* reported that a school district near Austin, Texas banned the novel because it "contains too much graphic violence, racial bigotry, and sex." The article links *Snow Falling on Cedars* to other banned classics, including *Of Mice and Men*, *The Adventures of Huckleberry Finn*, and *The Lord of the Flies*. Interestingly, *To Kill a Mockingbird*, one of Guterson's sources of inspiration for *Snow Falling on Cedars*, has also been banned in some parts of the United States for its depiction of sex, violence, and racism.

THE FILM

Snow Falling on Cedars was made into a film released in 1999, starring Ethan Hawke as Ishmael Chambers, Max Von Sydow as Nels Gudmundsson, and Sam Shepard as Ishmael's father Arthur. Ron Bass, who wrote the screenplay for *The Joy Luck Club* and won an Academy Award for co-writing *Rain Man*, adapted the novel for the screen. Scott Hicks directed the film, his first project after the critically acclaimed *Shine*. Guterson collaborated with Hicks extensively on the project, from working over lines of dialogue to giving Hicks a tour of the islands, and Guterson has a co-producer credit for the film. He and Hicks worked together to fine-tune Bass's script, eliminating Bass's voice-overs in order to, as Guterson said to the *New York Times*' Rick Lyman, "let the images do the work." Robert Richardson, who has worked extensively with Oliver Stone and did the cinematography for *The Horse Whisperer*, uses irregular camera angles, including partial shots of faces. According to Betsy Sherman, who interviewed Hicks for the *Boston Globe*, the director's goal "was to create a sensory experience that mirrors the story's arc, which he describes as 'a gradual shedding of light on the dark'."

Like the novel, the film jumps from the present murder trial to different points in the past. Talking to Sherman, Hicks called these moments "simultaneous time frames" that are part of, as he said, "a language of how memory works." Voices and images overlap in both time and space. The effect simulates the working of memory, of one image leading to another. This technique comes directly from the novel, but it is more powerful with actual images and an emotional musical score: the book is sensual, but a film can appeal directly to sight and hearing. This one does so, even to the degree that other senses are touched as well. The viewer can almost feel the heat radiating from the flames of the furnace and taste the strawberries Hatsue eats. The narrative movement also works as it does in the novel, with courtroom testimony dissolving into personal memory. In some instances, such as a few courtroom scenes, voices become layered and inseparable, signifying the confusing yet overwhelming circumstantial evidence against the defendant. The scene recalling Ishmael's war experiences is particularly powerful; Hatsue's voice reading her letter rejecting Ishmael overlaps the sounds of bombing, and images of her face interweave with those of Ishmael in the water and lying injured on the beach. Like the novel, the film focuses on details, such as close shots of a bird, a fish, a cedar branch, or a face. The images of Japanese Americans, underscored by a stark drumbeat, being "herded" on to the ferry are very bleak and reminiscent of images of Jews going into concentration camps. Many images of faces, particularly those of Ishmael, Hatsue, and Kazuo (Kabuo's name has been slightly changed in the movie), are partly obscured, suggesting that these people can only be partly known — even that they can only partly know themselves. The cinematography conveys viewpoint as well with these partial images; as Sheriff Moran drives up to the Heine house to tell Susan Marie of her husband's death, the camera captures what the sheriff would see as he looks out the windshield. Geoffrey Macnab, a reviewer for *Sight and Sound*, described the film as "beautifully crafted, full of lovingly composed images of mountains, woods, water and mist. The intention here seems to have been to emulate Guterson's prose with equally subtle and self-conscious camerawork and editing." He called the film "some sort of experimental film poem" (although he did not consider the experiment successful). The comparison to a poem, however, is striking, as the film, like many poems, relies more on images and sensory impressions than on narrative.

The film takes some liberties with the text, though not very many. (In fact, its faithfulness to the novel is, according to *Film Comment's* Chris Chang, one of its stumbling blocks.) Sherman pointed out, for example, that it was Hicks's research that led to the inclusion of a high school yearbook in the film; this yearbook has empty spaces where the faces of Japanese-American students should be. Some of the more significant deviations from the novel include the beginning and the ending. The film starts before Kazuo's trial, with images of Carl in the fog lighting lamps and blowing a horn. Another boat takes shape as Carl peers somewhat anxiously into the fog, and Kazuo's dark, menacing face appears. The film then cuts to black and picks up the next morning with Carl's boat adrift. The following scenes show the discovery of Carl's body and a few events leading to Kazuo's arrest and trial. The trial itself starts after the credits. These preluding events orient the viewer to the plot, but the novel, of course, begins with the trial itself. This difference establishes the frame of the trial more clearly in the novel, while the film's opening focuses more on the relationship between Carl and Kazuo and sets up Kazuo as a more dangerous figure. In this way the film is able to portray more clearly the menace and inscrutability that the islanders see in Kazuo's face. The film's ending differs too, providing not necessarily more resolution but rather resolution of different matters. Nels Gudmundsson and Ishmael sit and talk after Ishmael reveals what he knows, and the impression is of a father/son bond. Nels praises Ishmael for being like his father, providing a sense of closure to Ishmael's struggle to fill his father's shoes. Linking Ishmael's passion for Hatsue to the community's intense racism, Nels remarks, "It takes a rare thing, a turning point, to free oneself from any obsession, be it prejudice or hate or even love." Ishmael's taking over Arthur's role as the island's conscience is furthered in the film by the Japanese Americans turning to honor him in court after Kazuo is released. Hatsue hugs Ishmael after the trial, giving him the physical contact that he wanted earlier and she refused—a resolution that does not occur in the novel and that undercuts the book's suggestion that Ishmael must find a way to comfort himself. Finally, at the end of the film Ishmael walks away into the snowy night, unlike the book, which wraps up the story with Ishmael imagining Carl and Kabuo's relationship and their lives and preparing to write about them.

In the film, Ishmael's mother knows about his relationship with Hatsue, giving a tangible sense of the intimacy between mother and son that we see only brief glimpses of in the text; her knowledge also undercuts Hatsue's claim in the novel that Ishmael's parents would object to their relationship. Ishmael's mother discovers this relationship simply by watching the way Ishmael looks at Hatsue; while his father takes pictures of Hatsue as the Strawberry Princess, his mother watches Ishmael's face. Nels learns of Ishmael's love for Hatsue in the same way. That the film makes the relationship known, even in a limited way, strengthens the idea of the forced intimacy of the community and opens up possibilities for understanding. That is, despite the walls separating individuals, it is possible to know another person through observation and empathy. Ishmael is not as alone as he thinks. Flashbacks near the end of the film of Carl drowning and Ishmael underwater during the war link the two men, and Ishmael develops the capacity to sympathize with Carl. He comes to understand how they were both victims of forces larger than themselves. In a deviation from the novel, neither his mother nor Hatsue tells Ishmael to get married and have children. Such direct giving of advice seems less important than their acceptance of Ishmael for who he is.

The film received mixed reviews and did not perform well at the box office. Almost all the reviewers praised the film for its glorious cinematography and impressive landscapes. The *San Francisco Chronicle*'s Edward Guthmann called it "the most meticulously designed film of the year" and said "[i]ts images are breathtaking and reverential, like the best of Ansel Adams' nature photography" (which is particularly fitting, since Adams photographed Manzanar and its internees). At the same time, the review described the film as "plodding and self-serious" and in particular expressed disappointment that the movie "never brings the viewer inside the Japanese American experience." Guthmann blamed this failure to some degree on the movie industry, claiming that "Hollywood has a habit of glorifying the white guy when it tries to dramatize racial divisions," citing *Cry Freedom* and *Amistad* as other examples. Most reviewers expressed much the same sentiments: praise for the gorgeous scenery but frustration with the slow plot. Stephen Hunter, in his review for the *Washington Post*, described the film similarly, but he added his approval for the pervasiveness of war throughout the film: "we forget too easily how the war lingered in our culture for decades." He also commented, however, that "everyone in this movie has issues; it's overdosed on point of view." *Entertainment Weekly*, while praising the novel, claimed the best thing about the film was "the precipitation." The magazine disliked the film also on the grounds that the plot gets "blurred." Part of the problem was the critics' inability to categorize the film as a mystery, love story, or philosophical exploration. Hunter called the movie "a noir thriller hidden beneath too much education." Chris Chang, in a review for *Film Comment*, also found problems with the film's attempt to do too much: "By the time the narrative threads of a murder trial, a forbidden interracial love affair, World War II, a Japanese internment camp, and the residents of a damp Pacific Northwest fishing village are woven together, you will be hard-pressed to explain what, if anything, is at the emotional core." This sentiment of course echoes critics' reception of the book, but critics—and audiences—seem more willing to appreciate genre-bending in literature than they do in film.

Despite the almost overwhelmingly universal criticism of the film, it fared better among art house critics. Louis Parks, a writer for the *Houston Chronicle*, mentioned *Snow Falling on Cedars* as well as *American Beauty* as an early candidate for an Oscar based on its reception at the Toronto Film Festival. The film was nominated for the Best Cinematography award but lost to *American Beauty* (which also won Oscars for Best Actor [Kevin Spacey], Best Original Screenplay, Best Director [Sam Mendes], and Best Picture as well as garnering three other nominations). Parks' review of the film praised its faithfulness to the novel: "The film's broad form is epic and artistic (perhaps sometime too heavily artistic), but Australian director Scott Hicks (*Shine*) keeps it personal by focusing on a central relationship, not the events." It is sometimes difficult to tell where a flashback begins and ends, and some jumps in time are hard to follow. The film also has its awkward moments, usually in dialogue. In my opinion, however, viewers willing to be patient and do interpretive work will find the film rewarding and powerful.

5

Further Reading and Discussion Questions

DISCUSSION QUESTIONS

1. In his essay "Surrounded by Water," Guterson writes, "I live on an island in Puget Sound that inspires the envy and loathing of mainlanders. The envy, I suppose, grows out of the delusion that islanders live an idyllic existence; the loathing grows out of the corollary delusion that islanders have retreated from mainland affairs, fled from the intractable problems of our time, taken refuge from the late twentieth century on a pleasant curve of sunlit beach." To what degree, do you think, do the stereotypes Guterson addresses hold true, in life and in *Snow Falling on Cedars*? Consider the mainland journalists in the novel as well as the FBI agents. And how might the advantages and problems of living on an island affect a writer?

2. Both Hatsue and Ishmael's mother tell him to get married and have children as a solution to his unhappiness. To what degree is this an appropriate solution for Ishmael? Of what does happiness consist, according to the novel?

3. Consider gender relationships in the novel, which seem to be extremely traditional. Are they as traditional as they seem? What difference does culture play in definitions of masculinity and femininity and their relationship to each other? Are the characters satisfied with their gender roles? Why or why not?

4. What is the significance of coincidence and accident in the novel: Carl and Kabuo running into each other the night after they discussed the land purchase; Ishmael's finding evidence to exonerate Kabuo; Ishmael meeting Hatsue and her father on the road? Consider Ishmael's final epiphany: "that accident ruled every corner of the universe except the chambers of the human heart." What is the role of accident in fiction?

5. Ishmael waits a day to bring his discoveries about the ship in the channel to the authorities. What is the effect of his taking this risk on the reader's feelings toward him? Is this a betrayal of our trust as well of as Hatsue's? What light does this act (or non-act) shed on his character?

6. We know very little about the jury of islanders, and they never get a chance to bring in a verdict. What do you think they would have determined? What does it suggest about the island mentality that we do not get to hear their verdict?

7. Could a relationship between Hatsue and Ishmael have worked out? Why or why not? What would their adult romance have been like and what problems would they have faced, privately and publicly? Ishmael wants them to get married and move to Seattle to avoid the prejudice of the islanders; would such a removal to the city help their relationship? What does Guterson seem to be suggesting about the possibilities for race relations in the United States? Can we compare this small, insulated island with the larger American community? Why or why not?

8. In his essay "Blood Brothers," Guterson describes his own experience with his friend Ani, a man committed to Buddhist principles and to restoring the Tibetan government. Guterson ends this essay by suggesting that friendship can overcome conflicts between Eastern and Western values; his friend writes to him, "You and I have a special bond . . . which transcends barriers of race and religion, and even the constraints of time and space." Guterson then indicates the influence this friendship has had on his own perspective: "Analytical, rational to a fault, skeptical about all things inscrutable — a modern Westerner in the bones of my being — I experience wonder and joy." Do any of the characters in *Snow Falling on Cedars* come to feel these bonds or learn these cross-cultural lessons?

9. What is Guterson suggesting about the role of the past in understanding the present? How does the structure of the novel support and/or create this understanding? Consider also the persistent aligning of the male characters with their fathers and their fathers' professions and goals.

10. In his interview with Linda Mathews, Guterson claimed that "*Snow* isn't an especially modern book. I don't read many modern novels. So how could I write one?" Do you agree with his assessment of his own work? Consider the structure of the novel, with its flashbacks and easy flow from one person's memories to another's, as well as the plot of the story.

11. Compare the film version of *Snow Falling on Cedars* with the novel. How does the director replicate the narrative structure of the novel? Which is more effective? What differences between film and novel seem most prominent?

12. Examine *Snow Falling on Cedars* in light of *To Kill a Mockingbird*. What significant changes has Guterson made in the plot

and characters? Why? How does Guterson's approach to racial hatred differ from Lee's, and why? What differences are there in the conflict between Japanese Americans and whites and that between African Americans and whites?

13. Compare *Snow Falling on Cedars* with Guterson's second novel, *East of the Mountains*. What issues remain constant? How does Guterson's writing style suit or adapt to different stories and different subject matter?

14. How do Guterson's characters define masculinity, and what problems do they face as men? Look at the men in *Snow Falling on Cedars* in light of the problems men face in *The Country Ahead of Us, The Country Behind*.

FURTHER READING

Vintage's home page for *Snow Falling on Cedars* provides biographical information, a brief history of the internment of Japanese Americans, reading questions, and suggestions for further reading: *http://www.randomhouse.com/vintage/read/snow*. Readers may be interested in Guterson's second novel, *East of the Mountains*, or in his collection of short stories, *The Country Ahead of Us, The Country Behind*. Given *Snow Falling on Cedars* multi-genre format, readers may find any number of related texts appealing. Coming of age stories include Harper Lee's *To Kill a Mockingbird* and Gabriel Garcia Marquez's *Love in the Time of Cholera*, both of which address racial or class divisions, as well as Ernest Hemingway's *A Farewell to Arms, In Our Time*, and *The Nick Adams Stories* and Cormac McCarthy's *All the Pretty Horses* and *The Crossing*. Readers interested in historical fiction might consider Guterson's mentor

Charles Johnson's *The Middle Passage* and *Oxherding Tale*, Toni
Morrison's *Beloved* and *Paradise*, and Sena Naslund's *Ahab's Wife*;
Margaret Atwood's *Alias Grace* and *The Blind Assassin* are historical
fiction that focus on mysteries. Sea novels include, of course, Herman Melville's *Moby Dick* as well as E. Annie Proulx's *The Shipping News* and Howard Norman's *The Bird Artist*, both of which
center on small, sea-oriented communities. Suggested World War
II novels include James Jones's *From Here to Eternity* and *The Thin
Red Line* and Norman Mailer's *The Naked and the Dead*.

  Authors who address the internment of Japanese Americans, often from a personal perspective, include Janice Mirikitani, Taruko
Ogata Daniel, Jeanne Wakatsuke Houston, Ferris Takahashi, Row-
ena Wildin, and Hisaye Yamamoto. Yamamoto wrote *Seventeen
Syllables and Other Stories* (1988) and her "Yoneko's Earthquake"
was one of the *Best American Short Stories: 1952*. She received the
American Book Award for Lifetime Achievement from the Before
Columbus Foundation in 1986. Janice Mirikitani, a third generation Japanese American who spent time in an interment camp with
her family, has written a collection of poetry and prose, *Awake in
the River* (1978), that protests racism and oppression. Her work also
explores issues of sexuality ("Bitches Don't Wait") and personal
history ("For my Father" and "Breaking Silence," about her
mother's testimony before the Commission on Wartime Relocation
and Internment of Japanese Americans). Her second volume is
called *Shedding Silence* (1987). Dwight Okita, whose mother spent
time in an internment camp, has written at least one poem in
response to that event, "In Response to Executive Order 9066: All
Americans of Japanese Descent Must Report to Relocation Centers"
(1983). Joy Kogawa's *Obasan* may also be of interest.

  For readers who want to know more about the internment of
Japanese Americans during World War II, there are a number of

non-fiction books and essays available. John Armor and Peter Wright's *Manzanar* (1988) contextualizes the relocation in terms of Anglo-American attitudes toward Japan and Japanese Americans and presents some political motivations for the internment. It also describes life in the Manzanar camp and includes photographs by Ansel Adams. *Beyond Words: Images from America's Concentration Camps* (1987), by Deborah Gesensway and Mindy Roseman, describes the internment experience through interviews and reproductions of artistic work produced by Japanese Americans during their incarceration. Gary Okihiro and Joan Myers' *Whispered Silences: Japanese Americans and World War II* (1996) similarly combines photographs with the words of internees as well as government officials. Nancy Gentile's essay "Survival Behind Barbed Wire: The Impact of Imprisonment on Japanese-American Culture During World War II" describes how internment destroyed many of the cultural values and structures of Japanese-American life, such as respect for one's elders, family loyalty, and an established patriarchy; Sandra C. Taylor's "Interned at Topaz: Age, Gender, and Family in the Relocation Experience" similarly explores the impact of incarceration on Japanese American culture, particularly the differences between immigrants (*Issei*) and their second generation children (*Nisei*). Personal accounts of the internment may also be of interest; Yoshiko Uchida's *Desert Exile: The Uprooting of a Japanese American Family*, for example, tells the story of a girl's struggle to reconcile her Japanese heritage with her life in the United States, complicated by her internment years. Ronald W. Yoshino's essay "Barbed Wire and Beyond: A Sojourn through Internment—A Personal Recollection" is another personal account of internment, this one from a male point of view.

Selected Works by David Guterson

"Blood Brothers." *Los Angeles Times*, 1 May 1994: 26+.

The Country Ahead of Us, The Country Behind. New York: Vintage Books, 1989.

East of the Mountains. London: Bloomsbury, 2000.

Family Matters: Why Homeschooling Makes Sense. New York: Harcourt Brace Jovanovich, 1992.

Snow Falling on Cedars. New York: Vintage Books, 1995.

"Surrounded by Water." *The Earth at Our Doorstep*. Ed. Annie Stine. San Francisco: Sierra Club Books, 1996. 54–61.

"When Schools Fail Children: An English Teacher Educates His Kids at Home." *Harper's*, November 1990: 58–64.

Interviews with and Biographies of David Guterson

Blades, John. "David Guterson: Stoic of the Pacific Northwest." *Publishers Weekly*, 5 April 1999: 215.

Guterson, David. *Current Biography Yearbook*, 57:11 (1996): 27–29.

Guterson, David. "Seattle's Son." *Architectural Digest*, December 1998: 50–56.

Hochman, David. "Roughing It." *Entertainment Weekly Online*, 23 April 1999. Available at *http://www.ew.com/ew/archive/0,1798,1/25628/0/Roughing+it,00.html*.

Lanham, Fritz. "Desperation and Its Rewards: Dogged ex-teacher's eight-year labor a literary success story." *Houston Chronicle*, 26 November 1996: 2–18.

Minzesheimer, Bob. " 'Snow Falling' Author Hikes Different Terrain in 'Mountains.' " *USA Today*, 19 April 1999: 1D.

Weeks, Linton. "In the Shadow of 'Cedars:' David Guterson's First Novel Casts a Pall on the Second." *Washington Post*, 3 May 1999: C1.

Reviews of *Snow Falling on Cedars* (the Novel)

Biswell, Andrew. "First Novels." *The Independent,* 22 July 1995: 6.

Gerrard, Nicci. "Snow Falling on Cedars by David Guterson." *The Observer,* 4 June 1995: 16.

Harris, Michael. "Sometimes, Even Good People Must Coexist With Evil." *Los Angeles Times,* 19 September 1994: E4.

Henighan, Stephen. "Red and Yellow Necks." *Times Literary Supplement,* 26 May 1995: 23.

Herman, Carol. " 'Snow Falling' Does Justice to Trial Fiction." *The Washington Times,* 23 October 1994: B7.

Howard, J. "Snow Falling on Cedars." *The Washington Post,* 16 October 1994: 8.

Hughes-Hallett, Lucy. "Looking Like the Enemy." *Sunday Times,* 28 May 1995.

Iyer, Pico. "Snowbound." *Time,* 26 September 1994: 79.

Kenney, Susan. "Their Fellow Americans." *The New York Times Book Review,* 16 October 1994: 12–13.

Mallon, Thomas. "Snow Falling on Readers." *GQ,* May 1999: 112–118.

Mantell, Suzanne. "The Rise of 'Snow:' HB, Vintage, Others Boost Guterson Novel." *Publishers Weekly,* 18 December 1995: 21–22.

Maryles, Daisy. "A Cause for Celebration." *Publishers Weekly,* 7 October 1996: 20.

Mathews, Linda. "Amid the Cedars, Serenity and Success." *New York Times,* 29 February 1996: C1.

Mendolsohn, Jane. "Kind Hearts and Salmon Nets: Snow Falling on Cedars by David Guterson." *Manchester Guardian Weekly,* 25 June 1995: 28.

Minzesheimer, Bob. " 'Snow Falling' Author Hikes Different Terrain in 'Mountains.' " *USA Today,* 19 April 1999: 1D.

Muchnick, Laurie. "Snows of Yesteryear." *Newsday,* 25 September 1994: 32.

"No *Snow* in Texas." *New York Times Upfront,* 15 November 1999: 7.

Pate, Nancy. "Murder Unveils an Island's Secrets." *Chicago Tribune,* 12 January 1995: 54.

Reid, Harry. "Exploring the Sound of Fury." *The Herald*, 3 June 1995: 9.
Sussman, Paul. "Forces Greater than History: Snow Falling on Cedars by David Guterson." *The Independent*, 4 June 1995: 37.

Reviews of *Snow Falling on Cedars* (the Film)

Chang, Chris. "Snow Falling on Cedars." *Film Comment*, 35:6 (1999): 2.
Guthmann, Edward. "Chill Beauty in 'Snow': Story of Love, Murder and Race Never Comes to Life." *San Francisco Chronicle*, 7 January 2000: C3+.
Hunter, Stephen. " 'Snow Falling:' Adrift in Atmostphere." *The Washington Post*, 7 January 2000: C1.
Lyman, Rick. "A Film Director and a Novelist of Like Minds." *The New York Times*, 19 December 1999.
Macnab, Geoffrey. "Snow Falling on Cedars." *Sight and Sound*, June 2000: 54.
Parks, Louis B. "Festival Shows Off Oscar Possibilities of 'Beauty' and 'Snow.' " *Houston Chronicle*, 16 September 1999.
Schwarzbaum, Lisa. "Snow Falling on Cedars." *Entertainment Weekly*, 21, 28 January 2000: 99.
Sherman, Betsy. "Exploring the Landscape of Remembrance." *The Boston Globe*, 4 January 2000: D1.

Works on the Internment of Japanese Americans

Armor, John and Peter Wright. *Manzanar*. Photographs by Ansel Adams. New York: Times Books, 1988.
Bloom, Lynn Z. "Till Death Do Us Part: Men's and Women's Interpretations of Wartime Internment." *Women's Studies International Forum* 10.1 (1987): 75–83.
Chang, Thelma. *"I Can Never Forget": Men of the 100th/442nd*. Tucson: University of Arizona Press, 1996.
Daniels, Roger. "Incarcerating Japanese Americans: An Atrocity Revisited." *Peace and Change* 23.2 (1998): 117–134.

―――. *The Decision to Relocate the Japanese Americans*. Philadelphia: J. B. Lippincott Company, 1975.

Gesensway, Deborah and Mindy Roseman. *Beyond Words: Images from America's Concentration Camps*. Ithaca: Cornell University Press, 1987.

Gentile, Nancy. "Survival Behind Barbed Wire: The Impact of Imprisonment on Japanese-American Culture During World War II." *The Maryland Historian* 19.2 (1988): 15–32.

Okihiro, Gary Y. and Joan Myers. *Whispered Silences: Japanese Americans and World War II*. Seattle: University of Washington Press, 1996.

Taylor, Sandra C. "Interned at Topaz: Age, Gender, and Family in the Relocation Experience." *Utah Historical Quarterly* 59.4 (1991): 380–394.

Uchida, Yoshiko. *Desert Exile: The Uprooting of a Japanese American Family*. Seattle: University of Washington Press, 1982.

Yoshino, Ronald W. "Barbed Wire and Beyond: A Sojourn through Internment—A Personal Recollection." *Journal of the West* 35.1 (1996): 34–43.

Young, Mary. "Setting Sun: Popular Culture Images of the Japanese and Japanese Americans and Public Policy." *Explorations in Ethnic Studies* 16.1 (1993): 51–62.

Further Reading

Atwood, Margaret. *Alias Grace*. New York: Doubleday, 1996.

―――. *The Blind Assassin*. New York: Doubleday, 2000.

Hemingway, Ernest. *A Farewell to Arms*. New York: Macmillan, 1957.

―――. *In Our Time*. New York: Scribner's, 1970.

―――. *The Nick Adams Stories*. New York: Simon & Schuster, 1972.

Jones, James. *From Here to Eternity*. New York: Scribner, 1951.

―――. *The Thin Red Line*. New York: Scribner, 1962.

Kogawa, Joy. *Obasan*. New York: Anchor Books, 1994.

Lee, Harper. *To Kill a Mockingbird*. Philadelphia: Lippincott, 1960.

Mailer, Norman. *The Naked and the Dead*. New York: Holt, Rinehart, and Winston, 1981.

Marquez, Gabriel Garcia. *Love in the Time of Cholera*. Trans. Edith Gross-
man. New York: Penguin Group, 1988.
McCarthy, Cormac. *All the Pretty Horses*. New York: Knopf, 1992.
———. *The Crossing*. New York: Vintage Books, 1995.
Melville, Herman. *Moby Dick*. New York: Bantam, 1981.
Mirikitani, Janice. *Awake in the River*. San Francisco: Isthmus Press, 1978.
———. *Shedding Silence*. Berkeley, CA: Celestial Arts, 1987.
Morrison, Toni. *Beloved*. New York: Penguin, 1988.
———. *Paradise*. New York: Penguin Group, 1997.
Naslund, Sena. *Ahab's Wife*. New York: William Morrow and Co., 2000.
Norman, Howard. *The Bird Artist*. New York: Farrar, Straus, & Giroux,
1994.
Proulx, E. Annie. *The Shipping News*. New York: Simon & Schuster, 1993.
Yamamoto, Hisaye. *Seventeen Syllables and Other Stories*. New Brunswick,
N.J.: Rutgers University Press, 1994.